Days of Fear:
A Lynching
in St. Petersburg

Published by St. Petersburg Press
St. Petersburg, FL
www.stpetersburgpress.com
Copyright ©2023

All rights reserved. No part of this publication may be reproduced, distributed, or transmitted in any form or by any means, including photocopying, recording or other electronic or mechanical methods, without the prior written permission of the publisher, except in the case of brief quotations embodied in critical reviews and certain other noncommercial uses permitted by copyright law. For permission requests contact St. Petersburg Press at www.stpetersburgpress.com.

Design and composition by St. Petersburg Press
Cover Art by Amy J. Cianci
Cover design by St. Petersburg Press and Isa Crosta

Print ISBN: 978-1-940300-73-3
eBook ISBN: 978-1-940300-74-0
First Edition

Dedications

Jane A. McNeil would like to dedicate this book to her mother, Lily Dishman Bangert, and to the Evans, Tobin, and Sherman families.

Jon Wilson would like to dedicate this book to the memory of those who died at the hands of parties unknown.

Foreword

As developers and politicians in St. Petersburg, Florida, build skyscraper apartments and condominiums, and redevelop neighborhoods once inhabited by African Americans, others want us to remember the sacrifices and violence African Americans made and suffered in this waterfront community. They also raise questions about justice. Jon Wilson and Jane A. McNeil remind us of John Evans, who was lynched in 1914 during the era of Plessy v. Ferguson and state-sanctioned Jim Crow violence. Florida is one of the states with the highest rate of lynching. Between 1865 and 1950, almost 6,500 died at hands of unknown white assailants who largely eluded justice, according to a 2015 report by Bryan Stevenson's Equal Justice Initiative. The documentation of the unsolved murder of John Evans supports the citizen activists who requested that St. Petersburg acknowledge the harm that took place on the corner of Ninth Street South and Second Avenue near Tropicana Field. Wednesday, February 24, 2021, is marked as the day the city officials recognized a wrong 107 years after John Evans's lynching. Yet the unknown details of the mob and state violence persist among the majority of the citizens, both new and old. Wilson and McNeil help us to remember the pain of being a Black man in a culture where whiteness, exemplified through an alleged rape of a white woman and concern about northern investors, was a dominant cultural construction long before a Minnesota policemen snuffed the life out of George Floyd with a knee to his neck.

Foremost, this book helps to address the trauma and silencing of injustices towards African Americans and shines a light on this dark history in this investor-driven land of sunshine. It further substantiates a national movement led by attorney Stevenson to call the United States to a reckoning of the extrajudicial murder of so many African American men, women, and children and the harm it caused. During a time when legislators and other politicians attempt to deny the role of whiteness in the law and critical race theory, Wilson's and McNeil's research adds to the literature of such sources as *At the Hands of Persons Unknown* by Phillip Dray (2013), and *Lynching and Spectacle: Witnessing Racial Violence in America, 1890-1940* by Amy Louise Wood (2011). African Americans who once whispered about this lynching, and others, now have supporting evidence of a loss of lives and dignity because of such investigative truth-telling. Therefore, this book should be read by all from school children to politicians to both understand the past and help heal the present.

As Wilson and McNeil document the lynching of John Evans by unknown persons, we need to remember that these traumatizing events have an enduring legacy of injustice without a true reckoning. The Equal Justice Initiative (2017) explains that "lynching—and other forms of racial terrorism—inflicted deep traumatic and psychological wounds on survivors, witnesses, family members, and the entire African American community." A few years ago, a former student reported that her great-great uncle, Jim Press Merriweather, had been lynched in Alabama. The lynching traumatized her family so gravely that they did not retrieve the body. His father told the lynchers, "You killed him; now you bury him." Merriweather's wife moved to New York City. Folksinger Woody Guthrie wrote a song but the family lives with the pain of this loss.

A video the student made (*https://www.youtube.com/watch?v=YUu8N-qULET*) reminds us that three generations passed before the family openly explored Merriweather's lynching. As humans, we grieve when deaths occur. Imagine one day your loved one is engaging life as a normal person and the next day becomes a spectacle with thousands surrounding the body as it is desecrated for the benefit of the mob. Similarly, John Evans's descendants still live. Perhaps many reside in St. Petersburg. What justice will they receive? Although the perpetrators are deceased, the epigenetics of trauma and the economic conditions of the survivors endure. Recently, I read a quote that suggests that forgiveness is not enough; existence must stand on the pillar of justice. Wilson and McNeil uncover the hidden story of John Evans and thus require the city to be more vigilant to address the long legacy of injustice among African Americans that expands beyond the lynched.

These authors help us to recognize St. Petersburg as a commodified land and the possible motives for the lynching of John Evans. The name of the city alone highlights the displacement of indigenous people and the power of a Russian émigré to name a coastal city in Florida that symbolizes his hometown in Eastern Europe. Since 1885, when Dr. W. C. Van Bibber of Baltimore, an investor and physician inspired by William Chase, announced to the American Medical Society that the Pinellas Peninsula was wonderful for health, St. Petersburg has existed as a land for tourists and investors. We may note that Van Bibber's son and his associates invested in the area in hope of setting off a building boom. Perhaps Van Bibber's and his associate Chase's interests were not altruistic. Likewise, we learn that Frank Sherman, the man whom John Evans allegedly killed, moved to St. Petersburg for his fortune; he was a photographer turned real-estate developer.

Wilson and McNeil show that the past is intertwined with the present. Epistemologically, St. Petersburg's historical relationship with African-descended people is shaped by a philosophy of anti-blackness. St. Petersburg's city officials restricted by law in 1931 where blacks and whites could live and denied African Americans the right to swim at certain beaches as white investors, tourists, and residents arrived. Although people are not lynched today in St. Petersburg, and an African Americans is the mayor, other means are used to ensure the continuity of St. Petersburg as a commodified white public space. African American residences on the land where the Tropicana Field stadium stands, and the adjacent neighborhood where Laurel Park once stood, exist only in memory. Furthermore, ground-penetrating radar reveals that graves of African Americans lie beneath the parking lots 1 and 2 of Tropicana Field (TampaBay.com August 10, 2021), a stone's throw from where Evans's body hung from the light pole. The continuous disruption of African American life sometimes feels as though the segregation bar has not been removed. Now class bars the dreams of many African Americans. Homes sell well beyond the $33,033 median income of most of the residents, according to the 2020 census. Hence, housing for the precariat and the African Americans who sacrificed their land on unfulfilled promises, remain a distant dream. The *Weekly Challenger*, a newspaper that primarily serves African Americans, reports that July 18, 2019, at a community forum, 23-year-old Diguel Atkins, whose mother was displaced from Laurel Park, asked why affordable housing is so difficult when luxury housing dominates everywhere. Such highly leveraged price of housing and land intersects with the history of the lynching of John Evans. As concerns about frightening white developers away from St. Petersburg led the "leading citizens" to lynch Evans, so too Blacks are consistently relocated to accommodate developers and city planners' dreams of St. Petersburg as a white leisure space.

Additionally, we must not forget that the trope of Black men as rapists of white women drove not only the lynching of John Evans but also others in the United States. Ida B. Wells, a feminist journalist who became an anti-lynching crusader after two businessmen in Memphis were lynched in 1894, reported that the myth of Black men raping white women was designed to maintain white supremacy and establish white male hegemony (Davis, 1995). She observed that white men consistently raped Black women but feared white women's interest in Black men. Bryan Stevenson reports that lynching only ceased as states implemented the death penalty. Consistently more African American men are on death row. Had Evans not been a Black man, he probably would not have been lynched.

To appreciate the manifestation of a collective mob of 1,500 women, men, and children and state-sanctioned violence that led to the lynching of John Evans, the subsequent removal of African Americans and the continuous injustices they experience, it is necessary to understand the culture of whiteness. These authors provide context for the social connections that created such culture. Whiteness is property and property is whiteness, explains Cheryl Harris (1993). Frank Sherman's fellow developers killed Evans to guarantee that others would see St. Petersburg as a safe place to invest and live for whites, the authors reveal. Whiteness exists on a foundation of injustice that justifies extrajudicial actions such as lynching. The mob that lynched John Evans and the thousands of other African American ancestors knew, and continue to know, that whiteness trumps justice. Such investment in whiteness leads to the continual marginalization of African-descended people in St. Petersburg and around the United States and the material advancement of those who embrace whiteness. John Evans's lynching and the displacement of Blacks from the Gas Plant neighborhood are woven of the same fabric as evidenced by the background information Wilson and McNeil provide.

This book calls for a reckoning for crimes long overdue, truth-telling, and justice in St. Petersburg. Accountability has eluded the perpetrators; not one person has been tried, neither for Evans's murder nor for the other men, women, or children who were hanged during that period in the United States. It also raises the question, what is due to the African American community beyond a marker? Will the descendants of the perpetrators share the stories of their ancestors' participation? This book provides us more details that will help educate the public and bring healing and a reckoning to a past that is still present. I hope as developers, city officials, and new residents recreate a new St. Petersburg that they remember the lives lynched, displaced, and buried beneath the Tropicana lots.

Dr. Evelyn Newman Phillips, PhD
Central Connecticut State University

(Dr. Phillips was on the panel that created St. Petersburg's African American Heritage Trail.)

Preface

At a time when the Black Lives Matter movement has been embraced by an extremely diverse contingent of socially conscious individuals in America and around the world, and the MAGA movement is challenging all that American democracy and principles of due process rests upon, Jon Wilson's and Jane McNeil's book provides the citizens of St. Petersburg and the nation with an account of how racism and fear led to the lynching of innocent African American citizens. It provides a case study on what responsible individuals and institutions should do to avoid mob violence, police corruption, and judicial malfeasance.

As a former police officer and Chief in the City of St. Petersburg, I implore all of its citizens, criminal justice personnel, and government officials to read the book and commit themselves to ensuring the travesties Wilson and McNeil expose are never repeated, either by lynching in the traditional sense or through other forms of police brutality and unjustified shootings. While informative, more importantly, St. Petersburg's sad history is prescriptive.

Dr. Goliath J. Davis III, PhD

Contents

Dedications *3*

Foreword *4*

Preface *9*

Introduction *13*

Murder *17*

Chaos *23*

Ambition *34*

Vigilantes *43*

Secret *52*

Spectacle *60*

Afterword *72*

Endnotes *76*

Acknowledgements *87*

About the authors... *89*

Introduction

Days of Fear tells the story of a lynching that tore apart St. Petersburg, Florida, a resort town not far from its frontier past. It explores the life of a quixotic traveling salesman whose relentless quest for satisfaction ended with his murder. It tells of his steadfast wife, always in the background, who followed her husband across the nation. It tells of Black men sacrificed to appease white residents fearful for their safety, worried about their money, and willing to kill to uphold the dominant society's racial codes.

In November 1914 someone brutally murdered Frank Sherman. Two Black men, John Evans and Ebenezer B. Tobin, had worked for Sherman. They immediately became suspects. Fueled by accounts in local newspapers, mobs ruled for several days. Vigilantes terrorized Black residents, invaded their homes, and scoured the countryside as they searched for the suspects. In the end, Evans was pulled from jail, marched down the main street, and hanged from a light pole. Hundreds of white men, women, and children watched. Many carried guns. They fired round after round into Evans's dangling body.

This book suggests that John Evans and Ebenezer Tobin did not kill Frank Sherman. It suggests that a dubious accusation and an inflammatory press, coupled with economic forces and the anxiety of influential white men, doomed Evans and later rushed Tobin to the gallows.

If not Evans and Tobin, who killed Sherman? It remains a mystery more than a century later. This book's authors investigate it, offer a heavily researched narrative, and suggest a solution. Perhaps readers will come to their own conclusions.

The lynching episode survived as a footnote in the city's history but was seldom mentioned. "We always knew, but it wasn't talked about," said Gwendolyn Reese, president of St. Petersburg's African American Heritage Association. "We didn't discuss it as a family."[1]

Sometimes the city's white leaders denied that it happened at all. In the early 1980s, before the lynching began to be more widely recorded as local history, a high-ranking newspaper editor dismissed the incident as unfounded rumor.[2]

Easily accessible newspaper archives confirm the lynching. The reports, as the reader will see, issue a jarring account. It is relevant today because it defines a troubled racial ambience that has persisted for decades in St. Petersburg, where in 1996 riots erupted after police shot to death a young black man. It also threads St. Petersburg into a national pattern of violence that lingers well into the twenty-first century. There are many examples, a recent one being the May 2022 shooting in Buffalo, New York, where a white gunman shot thirteen people. Eleven of the dead or wounded were Black. Mob violence also continues. The January 6, 2020, attack on the national Capitol remains a fresh memory.

The Buffalo episode amounted to a mass lynching, belying the oft-voiced evasion that lynchers of bygone days were "men of their time." Says history professor Kevin Gannon: "The 'men of their time' excuse is exactly that: an excuse. An attempt to weasel out of actually reckoning with the past in all its complexity, violence, and shame. And it's fundamentally dishonest and ahistorical. People in the past did not 'accidentally' enslave others."[3]

In 1914, segregated St. Petersburg advertised itself as a serene and sunny spot. It was part of Pinellas County, which was formed two years earlier when the state legislature approved its secession from Hillsborough County. In a sparsely settled county where agriculture and undeveloped land dominated, St. Petersburg was the largest city. Its 1910 population was 4,127, with 1,100 Black people representing about 27 percent. In 1915, a state census set the population at 7,186. The city did not rank among Florida's most populous. It trailed such municipalities as Tampa, Jacksonville, Miami, Key West, Tallahassee, Lake City, and even West Tampa, credited with being the first suburban city to reach the top ten.[4]

But shadows stalked the Sunshine City, so nicknamed in 1910 by the afternoon newspaper's editor. Whites dismissed people of color as second-class citizens subject to contempt, arrest, and violence. As a St. Petersburg housemaid, alive in 1914, put it years later: "It's too bad to say, but we were just Black people, and they was white people, that's all."[5]

Microfilm from the November 12, 1914, front page of the *St. Petersburg Times* suggests an attempt may have been made to hide some aspects of the Evans lynching. A news story about the episode was indeed published on that edition's front page. But right next to that news story is an empty space where another article obviously was torn out, the microfilm shows. It raises questions. Could the missing article have contained information that editors or other city leaders thought might be further damaging to St. Petersburg's reputation, or possibly embarrassing to those who participated in the lynching? Newspapers elsewhere certainly stifled such reportage. A case in point is the Tulsa race massacre of 1921, in which newspaper accounts were removed before microfilming, according to history.com.

This book's authors searched other microfilm sources, consulted museum officials, examined other publications, and contacted private collectors. They did not find the missing *Times* clip.

To be fair, perhaps the article was about an entirely different subject and some interested party, heedless of historic integrity, simply clipped the piece before the page was filmed. The *St. Petersburg Independent*, the *Times* rival, offered detailed reporting of the lynching and the crimes that led to it. Nothing was clipped out of its editions. So these two newspapers (and others) recorded much for posterity. But still. The mystery of the missing clip continues to tease researchers. Perhaps it will turn up someday.

The City of St. Petersburg faced its past in 2021 when it dedicated a marker memorializing John Evans at the site where he was murdered. Then-Mayor Rick Kriseman spoke. "It is incumbent upon us as city leaders to call out, not just the injustices of today, but to recognize the horrors and injustices of the past as well," Kriseman said.[6]

The memorial site is near Tropicana Field, home of Major League Baseball's Tampa Bay Rays, and on the day of the memorial's dedication, Rays co-president Brian Auld also spoke. "It is ugly, it is horrifying. It speaks to the very worst of who we are and of what we are capable. But we cannot turn a blind eye to it, sweep it under the rug, ignore it. We cannot just move on and leave it in the past. That's what we've been doing for all too long, and it isn't working," Auld said."[7]

The co-authors hope this book provides a straightforward view of 1914 St. Petersburg, the tragic events that took place that year, and the forces that caused four lives to collide in deadly fashion. They hope it prompts reflection about the darker passages of the human journey and about the importance of seeking a brighter road.

The book also represents partial closure of a personal tragedy co-author Jane A. McNeil experienced. In a way, the book contains two stories. One is the 1914 episode; the other, suggested only in passing, is McNeil's journey toward co-authorship. Be sure to read her Afterword.

Documentarian Ken Burns has said: "Being an American means reckoning with a history fraught with violence and injustice. Ignoring that reality in favor of mythology is not only wrong but also dangerous. The dark chapters of American history have just as much to teach us, if not more, than the glorious ones, and often the two are intertwined."[8]

Perhaps there is no such thing as ancient history.

Murder

> *"Lynching is a vicious practice in which members of a mob take the law into their own hands. On the pretext of seeking retribution for some wrongdoing, they injure or execute a victim in summary fashion, at times with great fanfare and public acclaim. Presumptions of innocence and proof of guilt are treated as afterthoughts, if at all. The accused may have broken a law, violated a local custom, or merely offended prevailing sensibilities. Outnumbered and overwhelmed, the victim has no means of redress, since the mob functions as self-appointed prosecutor, jury, judge, and executioner."* [9]
>
> —Robert L. Zangrando

Frank Sherman went to bed early. Immersed in the mystique of Florida real estate, the 57-year-old entrepreneur had finished a busy day, and he expected the next few weeks to bring more hard work. Already it was November, and Sherman hurried to prepare his woodland acreage for the start of St. Petersburg's 1914 winter season and the expected influx of northern tourists who might be interested in buying property.

Two years earlier, Sherman purchased his tract on a desolate stretch of Johns Pass Road, which later became Thirtieth Avenue North. The tract began a few yards west of the Atlantic Coast Line railroad tracks. During the winters of 1912 and 1913 he and Mary Sherman, his wife, lived on Central Avenue in downtown St. Petersburg. Like so many others, the couple found the mild winter weather a comfort. They operated a photography studio. Each summer, they returned to New Jersey, where Sherman had studios in his hometown of Camden, and in the seaside resort of Wildwood, eighty miles away. Mary Sherman, 48, was also a professional, eventually advertising herself as "the popular child photographer of Camden" and an "Expert Lady Photographer" operating at Sherman's Sunshine Studio in St. Petersburg. The ads did not mention her husband's name. She routinely advertised as "M. C. Sherman" in the *Philadelphia Inquirer* and *Camden Courier*.[10]

It was among the piney woods and palmettos of remote Pinellas County that Frank Sherman, photographer, became Frank Sherman the speculator, dreaming of making his fortune. Many others in St. Petersburg held similar hopes. For three years, vigorous real estate trading had stirred the community, with property being sold and resold, often at inflated prices. Northern money provided much of the fuel for the little land boom. But after war broke out in Europe, financiers seemed to back away, and St. Petersburg's land fever diminished. When contracts for war materials finally began to bring new profits, St. Petersburg boosters anticipated a new wave of activity. As an editorial in the town's *Evening Independent* put it: "Now that the tight period is over the people of this city have bright prospects and there is every reason to believe real prosperity is coming."[11]

Edward Franklin "Frank" Sherman poses for a portrait circa 1912. The couple began wintering in St. Petersburg in 1912.

Sherman hoped the well-to-do would fall for Wildwood Gardens, the fanciful name he gave his property, which he advertised in the Wildwood newspaper, *Five Mile Beach Weekly Journal*, during the last three months of 1913. Marketing his development only in Wildwood, Sherman called his project "the newest suburb of St. Petersburg."

Mary Sherman's portrait suggests a Florida setting, as does that of Frank Sherman. Photos courtesy of Peter Stemmer/ Bassriverhistory. blogspot.com

In truth, the land was at least a half-mile from the nearest neighbor, several miles from the town, and still mostly bare. There was no running water, indoor toilet, or telephone. But Sherman had hope and a crew of eleven Black men clearing land and doing carpentry work. On the site was Sherman's home, a one-story, frame bungalow with its rear toward the railroad tracks, and a half-finished outbuilding to be used as a shed or garage. The waterfronts were miles away to the east and west. Neither Mary nor her husband belonged to a church or civic association. The couple had sold their business after two years and moved as far out of town as they could.[12]

November 10, 1914, a Tuesday, brought a soft autumn breeze, mild temperatures near sixty-five degrees, and a waning moon. According to Mary, her husband retired about 8 p.m., sleeping in a bedroom alcove with low, narrow windows on both sides of it and two larger ones in the front. Mary said she was sitting in an adjoining parlor making Christmas baskets of grass and pine needles. It was about 9:30 or 10 o'clock when a blast tore through the bungalow. Later, a newspaper would report that a powder mark was discovered on the corner of the house where the shooter apparently stood on a two-foot mound of dirt to aim a double-barreled shotgun.[13]

Mary said she ran screaming toward the bedroom. "My God, Ed, what is the matter?" It was then, she stated later, that a Black man appeared and stuck a revolver in her face. He threatened to kill her if she moved and demanded all her money. The first newspaper report said Mary's response involved throwing her skirt at the man with $102 in the pocket after offering him a check for all the money in the bank. Mary gave up the cash, which her husband had withdrawn from the bank the day before. But $75 was overlooked in one of Sherman's trousers pockets. According to Mary's account to police, a second Black man appeared, and the pair dragged her outside seventy-five feet from the house, beat her across the face with a length of pipe, battered her head against an outbuilding wall, and tore off some of her clothes. Newspaper accounts during the next two days strongly suggested she was raped.[14]

With a final threat to kill her if she moved, the assailants fled, and according to Mrs. Sherman, she fainted. The injured woman told police she regained consciousness a while later, crawled inside to her husband's bedside, touched his cold feet, and fainted again. When she recovered several hours later about 3 a.m. on November 11, she said she managed to put on a raincoat and crawl out of the house and across the yard and railroad tracks. She then got up and staggered a half-mile through the woods to the home of a friend, J. W. Richter. But the Richters, like the Shermans, had no telephone, so a boy was sent one more mile through the woods to another house, whose owner in turn sent his son to a Ninth Street house from which the police were notified.[15]

No longer serene

It was a shattering development for a town in which the peaceful pursuits of fishing, agriculture, tourism, and lately, real estate, had established a generally serene lifestyle—at least for white people. Black people, on the other hand, often led anxious lives because of segregation's strictures. Even a small misstep or a slight perceived by a white person might result in threats to a Black man or his family, or a jail sentence.

"One thing about this town . . . they lynched Negroes in St. Petersburg, but nothing like that happened in Pass-a-Grille," said Julius Bradley, whose family lived a while in the beach community. Bradley, 2 years old when Evans was lynched, said his family believed Pass-a-Grille was far from ideal when it came to race relations, but was a better option than St. Petersburg.[16]

The horrific crimes on Johns Pass Road scared and outraged white residents. Black residents feared the reaction of the white community. The shock waves jolted business leaders, who were counting on the support and money of affluent patrons who lived in and near Philadelphia—just across the Delaware River from the Sherman's home in Camden, where Sherman's mother and minister brother still lived. Newspapers in Philadelphia and Camden soon carried front-page accounts of the killing and the assault. St. Petersburg newspapers published lurid details. Said one account: "Police found him with the covers tucked around his neck, lying in a pool of his blood. His brains were spattered over the walls and the window opposite the one through which the shot was fired, was broken by stray shots." Reports also said the shotgun went off eighteen inches from Sherman's head.[17]

Through inflammatory crime coverage, such as the reportage above, American newspapers often helped instigate lynchings well into the twentieth century. A project called "Printing Hate," undertaken by two collegiate news organizations and fifty-eight student journalists, documented newspapers' roles in fomenting racial terror. Sometimes the instigation was inadvertent. Nonetheless, coverage did little to discourage systemic racism and often encouraged it.

DeNeen L. Brown, a *Washington Post* reporter and an associate professor at the University of Maryland, worked with the students. She writes about lynchings that the project documented:

"Some white reporters watched, took notes and wrote riveting accounts . . . as though they were writing about a sporting event . . . But those reporters, as skilled as they were as writers, often failed to practice good journalism . . .

"Many of these reporters failed to identify white people in the mob (or) hold government officials accountable by asking hard questions of the sheriffs, judges, and other local law enforcement officials who stepped aside while white mobs attacked Black people."[18]

Brown's descriptions fit virtually all the coverage of Evans's lynching by St. Petersburg and Tampa newspapers. No one among the lynchers or those who encouraged it had to answer for what they did.

Immediate suspects

Mary Sherman first accused a man named Carnage, but he had an alibi vouched for by several white residents. Mary then accused two other Black laborers, John Evans and Ebenezer B. Tobin, who also had worked on Sherman's property. She said her husband fired them after an argument. Both men later denied being fired, saying they had quit because there was no more work to be done. Law enforcement officials began tracking Evans and Tobin and did not investigate thoroughly to identify others who might have committed the crimes.

But the St. Petersburg Police Department and the Pinellas Sheriff's Office did not have much chance to delve. Their immediate task: restore order. Mobs almost immediately began scouring the county to find the two Black men. The hunt followed a pattern of brutality against people of color throughout the South and in many other parts of the nation. Participants typically felt free to act. The Center for Justice and Accountability cites a "legacy of structural racism . . . and the persistent lack of accountability and redress for centuries of violence."[19]

Lynching victims were usually Black. Between 1882 and 1968, 4,743 people were reported lynched in the United States, and 3,446 were Black. Florida accounted for 282 lynchings during that period, 257 Black. In 1914 alone, Tuskegee Institute reported that fifty-one of fifty-five lynching victims were Black. *The Crisis*, an NAACP magazine, reported even more victims that year—seventy-four, of whom sixty-nine were Black.[20]

An analysis of a slightly earlier period by the Equal Justice Initiative says Florida led the nation in racial terror lynchings per capita during 1877-1950, with 0.594 per 100,000 residents. During that period, Pinellas County had at least three reported lynchings; Hillsborough had five, Pasco six, Hernando thirteen, Sumter three, Manatee six, and Polk twenty. "Black men were more at risk of being lynched in Florida than any other state," University of Florida professor Jack Davis said.[21]

Chaos

"I will come again the morrow's way; and brush my fears aside."
—Frank Sherman

Within hours after the Sherman news spread through the community, white residents took to the streets and countryside. On foot, in buggies, on horseback, and in automobiles, men and boys carrying rifles, pistols, and shotguns began sweeping the southern part of Pinellas County. Searching parties were formed farther north after the news went by telephone to Largo and Clearwater. Determined posses with bloodhounds poked into the most desolate thickets of the Pinellas wilderness. In St. Petersburg, the chief of police ordered all saloons closed.[22]

The *Evening Independent* reported that two lines of men, one starting from Largo and the other from St. Petersburg, and stretching all the way across Pinellas County, were searching. Rumors flew, and each one sent vigilantes swarming to check. Reports that a bloodhound had been shot at Crystal Beach near Clearwater, and that three Black men had been chased into a swamp, sent a dozen packed autos swaying over bumpy roads to the northern part of the county. The shooting story proved false.

In St. Petersburg, rumors fed white crowds roaming the city's major streets. Many gathered at the combined city hall and jail downtown at Fourth Street and Second Avenue South, waiting for police to bring in suspects. Meanwhile, Black men were being brought to Mrs. Sherman for possible identification at Augusta Memorial Hospital, where a doctor was treating her. At intervals, throngs would dash to the hospital a half-mile away at Seventh Street and Sixth Avenue South. At one point, more than 100 armed men surrounded the hospital to prevent any suspect from escaping. Incidents of random violence began. As the mobs rushed back and forth, a man on horseback rode up to R. B. DuBois, a white man who was photographing the furious activity, and knocked a camera out of his hands.

But the vigilantes directed most of their terror against the Black community. To round up all the men who had worked for Frank Sherman, white crowds raided the Black neighborhoods west of Ninth Street and took a half-dozen men to the city jail. Officers arrested several others elsewhere, either on the strength of Mary Sherman's reports to police or because they were unfortunate enough to be seen outside. A group of white men returning from Clearwater shot three times at a Black man but missed. According to the *Independent*, no Black residents were physically harmed during the searches, but it was apparent many were psychologically traumatized. During the next few days, Black people left their homes carrying what belongings they could. Some took the train, while others walked the Atlantic Coast Line tracks north toward Pinellas Park and Largo. Their feelings and fears went unreported; newspapers recorded no comments from Black people.

St. Petersburg's days of fear had begun.

Flesh and blood

The people involved in extrajudicial violence were often depicted in reports as little more than stick figures with names attached. But John Evans, Ebenezer Tobin, Frank Sherman, and Mary Sherman, whose lives intersected tragically, were body-and-soul humans who displayed ambition, courage, and pride, even as their shadow lives may have concealed greed, deceit, cruelty, and murderous intent.

Information about John Evans and Ebenezer Tobin is incomplete. Southern newspapers of their era rarely mentioned African Americans unless they were associated with a crime. The Race and Slavery Petitions Project noted that "One of the inherent tragedies of slavery is the fact that the masses of Black people often remain nameless in the historical record."[23]

As an itinerant laborer, Evans would have been even further from a spotlight. A family tree shows Evans was born in 1883, the oldest of eight children born to Ella Jackson and John Evans the elder. That would have made the lynching victim 31 when he died. But his death certificate shows his age as 35. Between 1900 and 1910, he lived in Waycross, Ga., a starting point for many Black families who moved to St. Petersburg and other points south. Most accounts say that he came to St. Petersburg from Dunnellon, a small town near Ocala in Marion County. As a teenager, he worked in the nearby phosphate mines, which closed in 1901, leaving him to pick up work however he could. He came to St. Petersburg with Frank Sherman. The men somehow had connected in Dunnellon as Sherman was driving back from Jacksonville, where he had purchased a car. Sherman hired Evans as a laborer and chauffeur, suggesting some trust in the men's relationship.[24]

Ebenezer B. Tobin was born in South Carolina in 1871, according to the 1880 census. He lived a while in Ocala before moving to

St. Petersburg. A preacher and a carpenter, Tobin was the second youngest of eight children born to Patience Tobin. While growing up, he learned to read and write, a rarity then among Black people because educational opportunities often were limited for them. In St. Petersburg, for example, Jonathan C. Gibbs High School for Black youngsters did not open until 1927, three decades after the first high school for white pupils opened.

Tobin's father, January Tobin, born an enslaved person, served with the 104th Regiment, United States Colored Infantry, soon after the Civil War ended in April 1865. Also born enslaved, his mother was a farmhand on the Kilkenny Plantation, owned by John E. Tobin near Orangeburg, S.C.[25]

Always on the move

Frank and Mary Sherman led a nomadic life while Frank, a traveling salesman, relentlessly searched for professional and personal satisfaction. By the time they landed in St. Petersburg in 1912, they had moved ten times in their thirty-one years of marriage, including a two-year stretch in Ocean Park, California, a neighborhood in Santa Monica. There they lived in a luxury apartment complex, the Schermerhorn. After Frank's murder, the *Venice Daily Vanguard* reported that the Shermans were popular when they lived in Ocean Park, and that Frank was a sober, honest, and industrious man. "Sherman and his wife were most congenial people; therefore, they cultivated a large number of friends on all parts of the beach. Especially was Mr. Sherman well known about town . . . and those who knew him held him in high esteem."[26]

Edward Franklin Sherman, usually called Frank by friends and family, was born in the mining town of Pottsville, Pennsylvania on June 22, 1857. He was the second son born to two lifelong educators from small towns in Maine. He was restless, though some might have said flighty; he was intelligent, talented in certain ways, ambitious, and persistent in pursuing what he wanted at the moment. He wore a toupee. He smoked cigars. His hobbies were photography, gardening, and family history. Sometimes he wrote poems. In 1910 he sent one titled "The Optimist" to a Jacksonville newspaper. It expressed his determined spirit: "I will come again, the morrow's way; And brush my fears aside," Sherman wrote. He could also rush to judgment; the *Camden Post* reported that he had mistakenly accused a man of stealing his watch before recanting his accusation. Sherman had been visiting saloons at the time of the incident.[27]

According to school records, Sherman's father, Josiah Patterson Sherman, attended Bowdoin College in Brunswick, Maine for one year but did not graduate.

Frank Sherman's father, Josiah Sherman, was a respected college-level educator. He is shown in an 1868 photo. Photo courtesy of Peter Stemmer/Bassriverhistory.blogspot.com

Josiah did well in his career. Within five years after joining a high school faculty, he became its principal. After one year, he was elected superintendent of Pottsville high schools. In 1868 at the age of 46, Josiah became president of the Pennsylvania Female College in Collegeville. Less than two years later, he resigned and became the president of an all-female college, Tuscarora Seminary in Juniata, Pennsylvania.

Sherman's mother, Malvina Sherman, was said to be an exceptionally talented woman who read and painted without glasses at the age of 84. She helped Josiah manage schools while giving birth to four children.

Education was important to the Shermans. Three of their offspring attended school beyond high school. Adelaide, the oldest and only surviving daughter of the Shermans, received her Bachelor of Arts from Tuscarora. Eugene, who attended Freeland Seminary on the same campus, also graduated. Frank Sherman, who attended two years of college, entered the work force and found a career in the booming sewing and textile industry.

At age 23 in 1881, Sherman became manager of a sewing machine store in Chester, Pennsylvania, a town of textile mills and factories. It was sometimes referred to as a "saloon town" because of drugs, alcohol, gambling, and prostitution. Sherman lived in boarding houses and placed his first ad as a young businessman. It read: "If you want to purchase a sewing machine, you would do well to call at 121 West Third Street and see the Household. Frank Sherman. Manager."[28]

An ironic robbery

Less than two weeks after Sherman's ad was placed in the local paper, two robbers held him up at gunpoint as he traveled in a wagon on a dirt road. The highwaymen tore Sherman's shirt, roughed him up, and stole $90 of his employer's money. He could not give the police a description because his glasses were broken during the scuffle. It was reported he looked no worse for wear from the incident. The episode's details bore an odd resemblance to those Mary Sherman reported years later after she was assaulted in St. Petersburg. Both assaults happened in the late evening; both victims had their glasses broken; both were roughed up and had their clothing torn; both had a similar amount of money stolen; neither could immediately identify their assailants except to say one was short; and the assailants threatened both with a revolver.

As a young man, Frank joined the work force rather than opt for college. In 1879, the Williamsport, Pennsylvania, Star of Hope, a temperance journal, published an article about Sherman being elected as State Lecturer of Pennsylvania for the Patrons of Temperance. Photo courtesy of Peter Stemmer/ Bassriverhistory.blogspot.com

Despite the robbery, Sherman stayed in his Chester job until he returned to his parents' home, now in Elwood, New Jersey, in November 1883. It is uncertain how he met Mary Carroll Platt, but Sherman may have been a tutor at the small school in her tiny town of Harrisville or traveled on an errand for his father and met her. Harrisville was located deep in the woods known as the Pine Barrens. It had a population of seventy-five. As Mary wrote, the closest towns were all at least twelve miles away. Whatever the circumstances of their meeting, Mary and Frank fell for each other and married. In the church records, she is listed as 17 at the time of her nuptials. Frank's employment is listed as a teacher.

The couple moved to St. Albans, Vermont where Sherman found work for a new company, Singer Sewing Machines. But it was not long before he got into an acrimonious and very public dispute with a former employee. Each accused the other of dishonest dealing. Within a year, Ed and Mary moved again, this time to a succession of cities in Canada—Ottawa, London, Chatham, and Strafford. By 1888, the couple had returned to the states, living in the town of Jackson, Michigan. After two years, Sherman left Singer and moved to St. Joseph, Missouri, to work for a Singer competitor, White Sewing Machine Company. For the next dozen years, the couple would move regularly to start again in a new town. Unworldly Mary, who in a sense married "up," was exposed to a life she never would have experienced had she stayed in her hometown of Harrisville.

In St. Joseph, Frank Sherman acted as an informant in a crime. On March 18, 1890, a former Illinois State Senator, D.B. Gilham, was shot in his home in the middle of the night. He died from his wound weeks later. When the culprits escaped in the night, the senator's son posted a $500 reward for information leading to the arrest of the guilty parties. A year later, Sherman went to the authorities and offered them information about a former employee. The employee, J.R. Wyatt, was a bad character who often was in trouble with the law. When the police arrested Wyatt in Nebraska, he implicated two other men for the crime in exchange for his freedom. The accused men were known gamblers, one from a good family. Even though both denied the charges, Sherman's and Wyatt's testimonies caused the jury to find them guilty. Both men were sent to prison for murder. Sherman sued Gillham's estate to get the reward money and won. This might have given him the start-up money he needed to open the Crystal Type Photograph Company, making him for the first time his own boss. But the lawsuit made potential enemies for Sherman.

Sherman a government agent?

It is possible that he had made other enemies during his diverse career. At least one newspaper suggested Sherman had at one time been a government agent. St. Petersburg and Tampa newspapers did not mention the possibility. But an article in the February 12, 1891, St. Joseph, Missouri, *Herald* said: "Mr. Sherman . . . has had considerable experience in running down crooks, having done some for the United States government, and who was highly recommended for a consular position under the present administration by the secret service department at Washington."[29]

The newspaper article may have been inaccurate, perhaps based on inflated accounts from Sherman. But correspondence suggests Sherman did serve in some capacity for the government. He had written to United States Secretary of State James G. Blaine and to E. W. Halford, President Benjamin Harrison's private secretary, asking to be based in Wallaceburg, Ontario. Sherman received no replies. In a curious closure to the Halford letter, Sherman wrote: "Please give me an early reply (and) direct my movements, *I shall always remember you.*" Sherman underlined the last five words; one wonders if they were words of appreciation or a declaration carrying a veiled threat.[30]

Sherman also asked for help from a Secret Service official he had met during an investigation. But he hit a dead end again, although cordiality marked communication between the two. "My dear friend," began the letter to Sherman from John P. Brooks of the United States Treasury Department's Secret Service Division. Wrote Brooks: "I can assure you the receipt of your letter affords me much satisfactory joy, for your conduct in the St. Albans matter to my mind stamped you as of the few who are willing to do the duty of a citizen without expectation or hope of reward. God bless you." Added Brooks: "Kind regards to your wife."[31]

But Brooks gracefully turned down Sherman's request for help. "I am at a loss to reply to your request for information as to best course to pursue. I have never advised any person nor have used any effort to obtain a position for anyone," Brooks wrote.[32]

It must have been a blow to 33-year-old Sherman's ego. He had been accustomed to receiving high praise from employers during his varied career. A box of letters at the National Archives contains several recommendations. A typical one said: "I believe (Sherman) to be thoroughly upright, honest, and reliable and well qualified to fill any position of honor and trust either under the Government or private individuals." It was signed by two men, James B. Nixon, Member for

Atlantic County, State of New Jersey Assembly, and P. J. Byrnes, Judge of Common Pleas, Atlantic County.[33]

Such approbation doubtless buoyed Sherman during his unflagging search for satisfaction through New York, New Jersey, Pennsylvania, Michigan, Missouri, Illinois, California, and parts of Canada. Mary followed him everywhere. But her husband never found what he wanted, and eventually the Shermans moved back to Camden.

There, Sherman reinvented himself and switched careers. He became president of his Crystal Type Photograph Company, where he hired his own salesmen. Sherman continued to fight publicly with competitors, but for the next seventeen years, he expanded his business by advertising frequently and constantly promoting his photography over his wife's, while dabbling in real estate ventures, trying the postcard business, exploring his family history, and even thinking about starting a farming venture.

^ *Potential clients pose near the Sherman photo studio on the busy Wildwood boardwalk. Photo Courtesy of Kathi Johnston, Wildwood Historical Society*

Mary Sherman's transformation

Meanwhile, Mary Sherman continued to work on her own, getting photos published in newspapers, including the *Philadelphia Inquirer*.[34]

In her early days, Mary was a small-town teenager, uneducated and unsophisticated. She had transformed herself into an untraditional, determined, and ambitious urban woman during the Victorian Era, when women were expected to focus on child-rearing and domestic duties.

She was born on June 27, 1866, to Ann Eliza and William Hervey Platt at their family home in Philadelphia. Birth, baptismal, and other records identified Mary as Emma Louise Platt until 1880. That year, the federal census listed her as Mary C. (Carroll) Platt living in Bass River, N.J. The reason for the name change is uncertain. She continued to use the middle initial through the rest of her life. It helped define her as a strong woman with her own identity.

Mary Sherman changed herself from a small-town teenager to an untraditional woman in the Victorian Era. Photo courtesy of Peter Stemmer/ Bassriverhistory.blogspot.com

Mary's father enlisted in the Union army in 1862 at the age of 27 and fought against the South with the 95th Pennsylvania Volunteer Infantry Regiment in the Civil War's Battle of Gettysburg in 1863. Platt was a bookbinder when he and Ann Eliza married in 1857. Their first daughter, Emma C., died of the flu in 1860 at the age of 5 months.

Mary's birth name honored the memory of her dead sister.

Platt returned from the war a different man. Injured by a gunshot wound in the hip and leg, he walked with a limp and felt the pain of the wound long after it healed. By 1869, Platt had left Philadelphia with his family and chosen a remote part of the Pine Barrens to raise his three children. By 1880, the family had grown to seven with the birth of their two daughters. One daughter was what was referred to as an "idiot" with special needs. Platt's soldier's pension was used for her permanent care. So now the Platts had lost a child and their income was reduced because they had to care for a mentally challenged daughter. As if his suffering in life had not been enough, Mary's father died of gangrene from a botched corn removal in 1910. He was 75 and had outlived his wife and only son.

As an adult, Mary was determined to pursue a career. Like her husband, she became a photographer and embraced the craft as a vocation. She relished her role as a businesswoman and made sure to get an occupational license as a photographer in St. Petersburg during 1913-1914. She placed newspaper ads in St. Petersburg papers, calling herself "the popular child photographer of Camden, New Jersey." She learned to drive. She began forging a life of her own during an era when women's rights were few and society's norm expected them to stay home as dutiful wives. They could not even vote; the Nineteenth Amendment to the United States Constitution guaranteed women's suffrage, but it was still several years from passage.[35]

Mary's love of children was evident, as is shown here with her rector's daughter. However, she and Frank left the church for unknown reasons. She would rejoin the Methodist Episcopal Church while living in Haddonfield, New Jersey, six years after the death of her husband. Photo courtesy of Peter Stemmer/Bassriverhistory. blogspot.com.

For whatever reason, the couple remained childless, and when Frank opened a second studio, Mary was able to supervise a growing number of employees. The experience empowered her and began to earn her respect from male peers. Sometimes she traveled with a female assistant while Frank stayed at home. She managed her own real estate and placed want ads to barter items in her home for photography equipment she could not otherwise afford.

A pattern of violence stalked the Sherman couple's lives. Seven years before Frank's murder, Mary experienced horror in Gloucester City, Pennsylvania, when a man she was walking with stepped in front of a train and, as a newspaper article put it, "was literally ground to pieces . . . the fragments of the body were gathered up and placed in a pile." Peter Antonia, the victim, apparently heard neither the high-speed train's whistle nor the warnings Mary said she called out.[36]

Ambition

"Capitalists in Philadelphia plan to make St. Petersburg one of the most important ports in the South Atlantic states."
—Philadelphia North American

Men of influence successfully cultivated a bright image for their city. For example, in 1910, *Evening Independent* editor Lew B. Brown vowed to give away free newspapers any day the sun did not shine. St. Petersburg became the "Sunshine City" and Brown's flash of genius beamed worldwide. It became part of the city's self-image: sunny, cheery, peaceful, a perfect place for northern visitors, especially during the winter months.

In the years immediately before World War I, St. Petersburg was no longer a remote, pastoral village. Perhaps overly optimistic, it wanted to see itself as polished and charming. Women wore their hair bobbed fashionably short; colorful dresses with a straight silhouette were in style, while more daring women might wear harem pantaloons. Men embraced three-piece suits, narrow ties, and derby hats. Both genders still wore high-button shoes, though men were starting to step into the low-cut oxford look.[37]

On January 1, 1914, aviator Tony Jannus provided a thrilling start to the year by flying to Tampa from St. Petersburg. His feat was declared the first scheduled commercial airline flight. Photo Courtesy of Florida Memory, Florida State Archives.

But duality prevailed, as a news item in the *Independent* illustrated: A driver hauling state-of-the-art construction steel for the town's new gas plant was injured when the mules pulling his old-fashioned wagon bolted and ran away. Such divided character was evident in many ways. Wets versus drys fueled public acrimony as the two sides clashed over saloons and other aspects of local prohibition. (The Eighteenth Amendment prohibiting sale of alcohol nationally was seven years away.) Aviator Tony Jannus achieved the world's first scheduled commercial flight on New Year's Day, 1914, flying to Tampa from a piece of land on the approach to the city pier. Central Avenue was hard surfaced in the downtown business district and twenty-five miles of trolley track stretched to the outlying communities of Gulfport, Big Bayou, Coffee Pot Bayou, and west to the Jungle neighborhood on Boca Ciega Bay. But citizens wrote irate letters to the editor, complaining that the mule-drawn wagons were ruining the town's few blocks of brick paving. Mechanics in five garages fixed the growing number of automobiles, but there was still a livery stable, a harness shop, and three blacksmiths. Residents could keep cows in their yards for a $1 permit fee, and yet the town boasted a $150,000 opera house, reputedly the most modern south of Washington, D.C.[38]

The tranquil scene at the Roser Park bridge on Ninth Street South was a few blocks south of the site where John Evans was lynched. For a short time, vigilantes hid Evans in a house a short way east of the bridge. Photo Courtesy of Florida Memory, Florida State Archives

Not quite utopia

An *Independent* editorial in October 1914, bemoaning a recent increase in burglaries, noted that "St. Petersburg is getting out of the village class and is becoming a city." The opinion piece had it right. St. Petersburg was not the peaceful, small-town utopia its promotional literature claimed. A few months before the lynching, a murder case was said to have "stirred (the city) like no other case has ever done." William M. Boone's mutilated body was pulled from Reservoir Lake (eventually renamed Mirror Lake) on May 12, two days after he disappeared from his boarding house on Sixteenth Street North. Boone was employed as a watchman in St. Petersburg and was a nurseryman and farmer in his hometown of Versailles, Kentucky. A man called Judson Kennedy was accused of the murder, which took place just inside an alley on Fourth Street North between Fourth and Fifth Avenues, about two blocks from the lake. In another killing, John S. Dixon slit the throat of Andrew Gates.[39]

"Amateur and professional sleuths are working themselves down seeking to unravel the (Boone) mystery and it remains the most puzzling crime of the year in Florida," an out-of-town newspaper reported. County attorney W. R. Rowland took charge of the investigation and said the murder "in the very heart of the city is a blot on the name of the city and county." Declared the *St. Petersburg Daily Times*: "Never in the history of St. Petersburg was there such interest in a local story."[40]

Good news about local schools provided upbeat counterpoint to the grim murder cases. State education officials visited with an eye toward accrediting St. Petersburg High School with the Southern Association of Colleges. The school's enrollment hit 200, up from 184 the previous year, and the basketball team, temporarily practicing at the city hall, expected a good season.[41]

Southland Seminary opened in the downtown Manhattan Hotel, which would be used for classes until construction on the seminary building on Coffee Pot Bayou was completed. Kenflora College Preparatory School at 510 Third Avenue South offered high school, grammar, and primary departments. Said to be the only Montessori program south of Atlanta, the St. Petersburg Open Air School held classes at all levels. Mrs. Grant Aiken ran it at 456 Bay Street North. The school's newspaper ad noted that tubercular students were not accepted. All the schools served whites only.[42]

Meanwhile, St. Petersburg had developed a socially elite white society nurtured by the attention given the town by affluent and influential easterners, many of them from Philadelphia. Thanks, for example, to Philadelphian F. A. Davis and his companies, St. Petersburg had its trolleys, paved streets, and power company. The St. Petersburg Investment Company, a Davis brainchild to finance development in the town, attracted many other Philadelphia money men, among them George Gandy, H. C. Hatchett, William C. Haddock, Cyrus S. Detre, H. K. Heritage, Jacob Disston, and Charles R. Hall. During 1912-13, Gandy built the Plaza theater, which included the opera house and office buildings, on Central Avenue and Fifth Street. As early as 1906, the Philadelphia group had entertained big plans for St. Petersburg. That year a *St. Petersburg Daily Times* story mentioned an article in the *Philadelphia North American* that asserted, "Capitalists in Philadelphia plan to make St. Petersburg one of the most important ports in the South Atlantic states."[43]

Early St. Petersburg's downtown Central Avenue reflects the young community's duality. The trolley runs beside a parked buggy and an early power plant releases smoke on the waterfront. Photo courtesy of Florida Memory Project, Florida State Archives

Business ambition did not thwart good times. Plenty of leisure activity entertained white residents and tourists both. Boat excursions earned great popularity, with the Favorite Steamship Line offering daily trips to Tampa and points south along the Manatee River. Billed as especially speedy, the *Genevieve* promised a fast trip to Tampa from the foot of First Avenue North. Bridges to the Gulf of Mexico beaches had yet to be built, but the Boca Ciega Boat Company took passengers to Pass-a-Grille.⁴⁴

St. Petersburg's long love affair with baseball was well under way with its all-white team playing Florida League games at Sunshine Park, where for 25 cents admission spectators could see the St. Petersburg Burlies play teams from Tampa, Lakeland, and Fort Meade.⁴⁵

Card devotees regularly scheduled whist, bridge, and rummy sessions. The town band, eager to raise money for new uniforms, blazed away frequently downtown or on the municipal pier, soon to add thirty feet to its length and place a set of spacious benches for weary white people. The improvements, city hall promised, would make the pier the most popular feature in St. Petersburg. Black people were not allowed to visit it, and they were not allowed to use benches elsewhere in St. Petersburg.⁴⁶

Busy businessmen

Business leaders constantly beat the drums. Board of Trade President Charles R. Hall and St. Petersburg Investment Company manager H. Walter Fuller, returning from a conference in Philadelphia with St. Petersburg investors, reported high optimism among the easterners, who were said to be loosening their finances. "Each brings a story of prosperity that will not much longer be delayed," exulted an *Independent* editorial. "They say St. Petersburg's prospects are better than ever and they are in a position to know, for they are the men who do things." The *St. Petersburg Times* urged every citizen to get behind improvements: "So don't growl. Boost! Boost, durn you! BOOST!" (The comment, including the upper-case letters, appeared on a *Times* opinion page.)⁴⁷

Hall, who had a reputation as a master salesman, claimed that people would be sleeping in bathtubs for lack of better accommodations. He reported also that $100,000 worth of property had been sold to prospective winter residents during early autumn, at a rate of one home per week. W. A. Huber, president of the Pennsylvania State Society, announced that he expected to "bring a good-sized party (of visitors) with me to St. Petersburg this winter." Another St. Petersburg resident, recently returned from a northern trip, reported that railway and steamship offices in Boston had never seen such large bookings for Florida and that ninety percent of them were for the state's West Coast.⁴⁸

Whatever the season brought, 1914 had been a landmark year for St. Petersburg. The new gas plant and garbage crematory were almost complete. Nine miles of gas mains had been laid, although supervisor

F. J. Stamm worried about the theft of red lanterns used at night to mark street work. A second railroad, the Tampa and Gulf Coast, was building a $20,000 depot in town and expected to begin St. Petersburg service soon. A Carnegie library was under construction. An agreement was reached to bring the Philadelphia Phillies to town for spring training in 1915. Western Union added a new wire in anticipation of highest business in the city's history, announced manager Mrs. Almon Vanlandingham, and a new telephone switchboard was being shipped. The city also received important support from the Atlantic Coast Line railroad, which devoted the entire back page of its fall promotional brochure to St. Petersburg.[49]

Smaller businesses hoped to benefit, too. Jack Williams advertised a "tonsorial parlor" at Central Avenue and Second Street, where you could shoot a game of pool while awaiting your shave and haircut. Citizens Ice and Cold Storage Co. daily delivered door to door blocks of ice—what the company called "a concrete blessing." The local citrus crop was said to be the best in years and growers tried to outdo one another in attractive packaging. In a bid to satisfy lingering Victorian attitudes, an undertaker advertised "lady attendants." A photography shop called Central Avenue Studio, 534 Central, was the agent for photo giant Eastman Kodak and promised to develop and print film in two hours. The Willson Chase woman's store advertised dresses in several colors, tastelessly describing one shade as "nigger brown." Such a reference would be a horribly unspeakable slur in future eras, but in 1914 it was casually dropped in a merchant's promotion.[50]

The town's two preeminent newspapers rarely mentioned Black citizens unless it was in connection with a crime. The Oct. 2, 1914 *Times*, for example, reported that "C. F. McLeod, a black man, pleaded guilty in circuit court to desertion and failure to support his wife." There were exceptions. In another edition during the same month, the *Times* noted that J. W. Ovletree had been elected president of the Negro Business League, which hoped to invite author, educator, and national Black leader Booker T. Washington to speak; the same item noted that Dr. C. R. Williams had marked his birthday. Such mentions were rare. Williams was a pioneer Black physician in St. Petersburg who was also among the first African Americans to attempt to vote in St. Petersburg. He died of a heart attack in 1927 while standing in line at a polling place.[51]

Strictly separate

Like most Southern towns, St. Petersburg was strictly segregated by race. Blacks, composing about one-third of the city's population, generally lived in separate areas west of Ninth Street, although the small neighborhood known as Pepper Town thrived east of Ninth Street along Second, Third, and Fourth Avenues South. The largest sections were "Cooper's Quarters" near the gas plant project just west of Ninth Street South, "Methodist Town" north of Central Avenue and another settlement about a mile west of the city limits near a trail that became Twenty-Second Street South. The Black sections contained their own churches, stores, and meeting halls because the residents could not shop or meet in white sections. Social life and entertainment revolved around churches and lodges. Blacks had a small hospital on Fourth Avenue South near Eleventh Street, and their own schools, the main one being Davis Academy on the eastern edge of Cooper's Quarters. It was named for Ned Davis, a white philanthropist who financed segregated Mercy Hospital on Twenty-Second Street South in 1923.[52]

There is irony in the treatment of African Americans as undeserving of the same amenities as white citizens. Blacks provided much of the work force creating a modern, attractive town with an appealing lifestyle for its white residents. Men worked as laborers for one of the town's twelve white building contractors on street-paving projects and on sewer-laying jobs. Others worked for the railroads or were craftsmen. Black women were waitresses, maids, cooks, and laundresses for hotels, restaurants, and the private residences of affluent white people. Other than the hours they spent working there, Black people were seldom allowed in the business district or in the white residential sections. In later years, the City Council tried to make these restrictions a matter of official policy. A city charter in 1931 included a clause banning white people from living or having a business in Black neighborhoods, while banning Black residents from doing the same in white neighborhoods. In 1936, the council approved a resolution to make African Americans live west of Seventeenth Street between Sixth and Fifteenth Avenues South. Both measures proved impractical to enforce.[53]

Segregation was enforced in the political process as well. In 1913, for example, a primary election in which only whites were permitted to vote produced the commissioners who would direct town affairs for the next several years. The whites-only election was called because some candidates apparently had strong support from Blacks. Lew B. Brown's *Independent* supported the white primary as "a voluntary expression of the white voters in order to maintain control of city affairs in the hands of the white people." It expressed fear that Blacks could control the town if all of them voted in a bloc. That five hundred Black people were registered to vote—less than one-twelfth of the town's population —seemed enough of a threat to the white community to justify the special primary.[54]

Elected were J. G. Bradshaw, commissioner of public affairs; T. J. Northrup, commissioner of public safety; and C. D. Hammond, commissioner of public works. A week later, Bradshaw was chosen mayor by the other two. Bradshaw declared before the election that he "wanted to go into office as the choice of the white voters of the city and would rather not have the office than to rely on the [N]egroes to win."[55]

Segregation had always been present to some degree in St. Petersburg, but to some Blacks it seemed that the practice grew harsher as the 1900s progressed. Paul Barco, a Black St. Petersburg resident whose father had arrived in 1905, recalled that his mother and father conducted their courtship in Williams Park downtown, but Barco, born in 1916, said he had grandchildren before he saw the park for the first time. The intensity of racial discrimination seemed to increase after 1905. Barco observed:

"My daddy said when he came to this city, if you had to go to a doctor, you went on over to the doctor. He had one waiting room there, he waited on whoever was there. And the people who were in there were rustic white people, just like the others who were Black. They were not the polished persons from elsewhere, who probably had never been around a Black person. But my dad said as these persons began to come down who had great amounts of finance and they had been exposed to a great deal of literary training, then these people felt that they didn't care to sit in the same room with these Black people."

According to his father, "the polished persons" put pressure on the people who rendered the services to establish separate facilities. Eventually, the doctor, who was white, added a separate waiting room for Black people, telling Barco's father that "things were changing."[56]

Even petty crime committed by Black people frequently resulted in a harsher response. Whites would not hesitate to shoot at a Black person for so slight a transgression as stealing fruit out of a grove. Such extreme reaction for minor offenses further defined a system that placed people of color in an inferior position that seldom accorded them the consideration a white person would enjoy. Interviewed late in her life, the maid Lula Grant emphasized the point repeatedly. "We weren't considered any way, we were just Black people," she said.[57]

Scrapping for influence

Politics provided an arena where prominent white men sparred for power. State and local elections took place in early November 1914. But the big story involved alleged corruption on the part of the county commission. A grand jury charged each of the five commissioners with malfeasance and misfeasance, and ordered the arrests of O. T. Railsback, F. A. Wood, J. T. Lowe, S. S. Coachman, and L. D. Vinson, with bonds for each set at $2,000. The grand jury cited county buildings in disrepair, very bad jail conditions, and a "regrettable laxity of official duty." Wood, who had announced his bid for the State Legislature, responded that the board had done nothing unlawful. Judge Leroy Brandon threw out the charges about a month later. The grand jury foreman was *Times* editor William L. Straub, one of St. Petersburg's most powerful men through his newspaper role and leadership of the Board of Trade, and now as head of the group deciding who should be charged with crime. Straub had made it clear he did not want to serve on the grand jury because of his position as editor, but to no avail.[58]

The *Times* was one of two lively newspapers in town, the other being the *Independent*. The two papers maintained a spirited rivalry, often sniping at one another in opinion columns. Feisty Lew B. Brown led the *Independent*.

Straub's *Times* carried on its opinion page the slogan, "Be sure it is right—then boost it," and the words seemed to provide inspiration. Residents consistently united behind proposals for improvements: More than $600,000 was approved by voters in bond issue elections from 1909 to 1913, and not one issue was defeated during that period.[59]

Earlier in 1914, city leaders printed and mailed at great expense more than 50,000 pieces of promotional literature. Only a successful tourist season could recover the money.[60]

Then disaster struck on Nov. 10. Frank Sherman lay murdered in his bed. Black men killed him, said Mary Sherman, his wife, who also claimed that the killers had assaulted her—a more horrendous crime in the minds of many white people. With only eight policemen on its payroll, the city was plunged into a situation where it was forced to cope with serious crime and civil disorder.

Vigilantes

"Evans was subjected to intense methods to provoke a confession but remained a stoic throughout."
—Tampa Tribune

From her hospital bed a few hours after her husband's murder, Mary Sherman told Dr. F. W. Wilcox that she thought she recognized the voice of one of her assailants as that of John Evans. He had been working several weeks for her husband and was a familiar figure around the couple's house.

Something went awry in the men's relationship, and Sherman fired Evans on Saturday, November 7. Several days after the lynching, Mary Sherman said the firing made Evans "greatly angered." She said Evans "mouthed" and accused her husband of not "playing fair." As noted earlier, Evans denied being fired, as did Tobin. [61]

Evans drank during the following weekend and seemed to carry a grudge. James Vann, Evans's roommate, said Evans left their house early on the evening of Sherman's November 10 murder and did not return until 4 a.m. the next day.

"He had some whiskey in a bottle and offered me a drink," Vann told the *Independent*. "I asked him where he had been so late at night, and he said it was none of my business and for me to go on and drink and let him alone." Vann said Evans also told him: "We're all in trouble."[62]

On November 11, a coroner's jury viewed the murder scene, as did Police Chief A. L. Easters. So did Deputy Charles Simms, representing Pinellas County Sheriff Marvel Whitehurst. The law officers believed that Sherman's killer had crept to a window outside the alcove where Sherman lay sleeping, stood on a low pile of dirt, and fired a shotgun through the screen. Footprints under the window seemed to match others leading north from the house. Mary Sherman offered descriptions of the Black men she said attacked her: One was tall and wore a black felt hat; the other was short and had a little mustache. Based on her statements relayed through Dr. Wilcox, Easters ordered the arrests of Evans and another Black man known as Tobe, said to have fingers missing on his right hand.[63]

A hardy woman

Mrs. Sherman's resilience amazed Dr. Wilcox. "The unfortunate woman has a remarkable physique, and only a perfectly healthy and very strong woman could have suffered what she did and lived," he said.

"A remarkable fact about this case is that, in spite of her injuries, she dragged herself nearly a mile from where the murder and other crime was committed and gave the alarm. Not one woman out of a hundred could have done this, and the blow she received would have been enough to probably kill almost any ordinary woman."[64]

As news of the crimes spread, residents began to mill in the streets, some forming search parties. The first person arrested was Ebenezer Tobin. Sheriff's Deputy Grover C. McMullen made the arrest on Ninth Street when he spied a man who fit the description of the man called Tobe. After questioning at the St. Petersburg police station, McMullen put Tobin on a train to Clearwater before anyone in the gathering crowd learned of the arrest. Tobin was held in the county jail at Clearwater even though Deputy Simms searched the Black man's home, found no evidence, and said that he believed Tobin told the truth when he denied any part in the crime. Authorities at first wanted him to help search for suspects.

McMullen also arrested another Black man, George W. Gadson, in some woods near Largo after two detectives trailed Gadson and three other Black men along the railroad tracks. John Evans was found about the same time by former deputy sheriff E. L. Proctor, with the help of a Black informant. But Evans could not be linked to the killing. Taken before Mrs. Sherman, he was released after she could not identify him as her attacker. Mrs. Sherman looked at several other black men but could not name any as an assailant. As Evans left the hospital, the crowd outside "took charge of him," said the *Independent*. "The [N]egro was closely questioned and then searched and told to go on his way. His release made the solution of the murder mystery more difficult," the newspaper said.[65]

While crowds dashed around town, grim manhunters prowled the rural areas, looking for suspects they thought must be hiding in the dense woods. It was rough going. George Gandy, one of the searchers, said the country his party went through was so thick with palmettoes that one hundred men could have hidden within a few feet and never have been detected.[66]

In town, Central Avenue remained crowded with white people until midnight. Blacks disappeared from the streets, even in their own sections, and nearby Ninth Street was empty except for an occasional car carrying white men. At the railroad depot, just one Black hotel porter remained on duty, although many were usually on hand to meet the night train.

A menacing posse

Thursday, November 12, began ominously. Frustrated after failing to find and identify the Sherman attackers, a posse raided Black homes during the early morning hours and took a half-dozen men to jail. Later in the morning, St. Petersburg seemed quieter than on the previous day, with not so much frantic running around, although the streets remained crowded.

As the day wore on, new developments began to excite people again. By now, both the morning and evening newspapers had devoted much space to detailed, sometimes gruesome accounts of the crimes, descriptions of Black suspects including their names, and the progress of the manhunt. Apparent confirmation that Mrs. Sherman had been raped further infuriated the white population. The *Independent* published an article pointing out that Florida law prohibited printing the name of a woman who had been sexually assaulted. The article also reported that it would be unlawful to mention the woman's relationship to Sherman, because it would identify her. Thus, the newspaper disclaimer, added to opinion in the community, effectively suggested that Mrs. Sherman was a rape victim.[67]

It was an excuse frequently—but not always—used to justify lynching Black men. African American journalist Ida B. Wells, who led an anti-lynching campaign during the 1890s, said that less than one-third of lynching victims up to that time had been accused of rape. She said the others were murdered under many pretenses, including "acting sassy." The real aim, Wells wrote, was to suppress Blacks economically through terror and violence.[68]

In an article for the website *Literary Hub*, Alex Tresniowski noted: "The lynching of (Wells') close Memphis friend, Thomas Moss, had, after all, been precipitated by an economic clash—Moss's Black-owned grocery posed a threat to a rival white-owned store. In the end, Moss's lynching led to the destruction of his store, and to its stock and customers being absorbed by the very rival who saw to it that Moss was lynched."

Economics also played a part in the lynching of John Evans, as St. Petersburg's Black residents were beginning to build a niche for themselves. Leaders such as J.W. Ovletree organized the Negro Business League, "desirous of putting the people of their race on a higher plane." A letter from Emmett J. Scott, a journalist and close adviser to Booker T. Washington, encouraged the entrepreneurs.[69]

Some applied for liquor licenses but were turned down on grounds that the petitions for the licenses were not properly signed and that "the applicants were not of good character," even as three new white saloons opened. "The rush for the white bars was like the scramble for free land in the West and the bartenders were swamped all during the morning," according to one report.[70]

The rebuff angered the Black businessmen, who believed they had been double-crossed. One unidentified Black businessman said: "We spent our money and got out the [N]egroes so that the county would go wet, and it would never have voted for saloons if the [N]egroes had not carried it that way. Yet we are turned down hard and cold and cannot get saloon licenses after all that we have done."[71]

White residents had long sought ways to intimidate Blacks economically and otherwise. The white-organized Good Government League went so far as to hire a detective whose purpose was to go into Black neighborhoods and scare the residents out of voting and attempting to better themselves financially. The lynching of John Evans on Ninth Street South next to a Black neighborhood was the extreme step in a long-standing economic intimidation campaign.[72]

Fanning the Anger

Although the *Independent*'s November 12 lead editorial denounced mob violence and expressed hope that the law would take its proper course, the news columns of both local papers continued to fan residents' anger. Besides graphic descriptions of the crimes, stories contained leading statements. For example, an *Independent* story said, ". . . the general feeling is that the guilty man should be hanged promptly as soon as positively identified." On the previous day, the *Independent* had speculated that the guilty parties, if caught, had small chance of getting to jail alive. City editor A. R. "Archie" Dunlap's November 12 column brought up the idea of lynching, although he stopped short of endorsing it. In an accompanying front-page story, the *Independent* reported that new clues had been found and that one of them appeared to link John Evans to the crimes. Despite his release the day before, Evans was still under suspicion because he had left Sherman's employ under forced circumstances, the story said. It also noted: "The general feeling here is that Evans knows more of the crime than he has told."[73]

Meanwhile, the St. Petersburg newspapers had gone by train to Clearwater and other sections of north Pinellas County. The news agitated residents in those sections. "They came in (to St. Petersburg) from all over the upper county. Old-timers, old pioneers, they came in on horseback," according to Luther Atkins, a St. Petersburg resident who observed the events and recalled them in an interview.[74]

Two discoveries again led manhunters to John Evans. A torn and bloody man's shirt and a pair of bloody shoes were found by a search party in the back of a house in Methodist Town where Evans had roomed. James Vann, a Black man in the house at first stated that the shirt belonged to Evans, but he later changed his mind, saying he did not know who owned it. Another piece of evidence also turned up. A double-barreled shotgun, thought to be the murder weapon, was found alongside the railroad tracks south of the Sherman home toward the town. One barrel had recently been fired, and the gun appeared to be the one earlier stolen from L. S. Hardee's home on Central Avenue. That discovery seemed to indicate the assailants must have fled south instead of north as originally supposed because of vague sets of footprints. But it did not immediately implicate any person. Nonetheless, the bloody shoes and shirt were enough to spur the search parties on another hunt for Evans. Though Mrs. Sherman had said the day before that Evans was not her attacker, her statements were now placed in doubt by authorities suggesting her injuries and medication prevented her from thinking clearly.

Since his release from custody the day before, Evans had gone to work for a Black man west of downtown near Fifth Avenue South and Twenty-second Street. Someone telephoned his whereabouts to Police Chief Easters. The caller also indicated that Evans had been told a mob was after him again, but he had responded that he would not run. If the mob wanted him, he said, it could come get him.[75]

It did so after receiving directions from Easters. Hoping to force a confession, the vigilantes took Evans into the woods, tortured him, and nearly lynched him on the spot. According to the *Tampa Tribune*, Evans "was subjected to intense methods to provoke a confession but remained a stoic throughout. After his continued denial that he knew anything of the crime, Evans was told to make his peace with God and to say his prayers. He said he had no prayers to say. It is alleged a rope was placed around his neck and he was lifted off the ground, but he continued to deny he is the guilty man."[76]

Unable to extract a confession, the vigilantes decided to take Evans into town so Mrs. Sherman could see him again. For a while, he was held in a Roser Park garage, a neighborhood just south of downtown, while an expectant crowd at the nearby hospital awaited his arrival. But Evans did not appear. The impatient crowd began to disperse, and Evans was then taken to Mrs. Sherman, who for the second time could not identify him. She said she could not see without her glasses, which had been broken in the assault. Dr. Wilcox said also that her vision had been damaged by the blow she had received across the left eye. Later, Dr. Wilcox, Mayor J. G. Bradshaw and Police Chief Easters talked briefly with the people outside the hospital, saying that Evans would be left in the St. Petersburg jail and not taken to Clearwater if the crowd would not molest him until he could be named as an assailant.[77]

During the afternoon, the crowds downtown grew more unruly. "A number of strangers, probably from the outlying sections, appeared and the crowd became more determined," reported the *St. Petersburg Times*, although the account noted that there was no talk of lynching or breaking into the jail. But at one point, a group at the city hall became so demonstrative that Mayor Bradshaw mounted the steps to plead. He contended that he had no doubt that justice would be delivered, whether by summary justice of some determined contingent or, as he hoped, by a legally constituted court.[78]

The vigilantes strike

About 10:30 p.m. on November 12, a mob that news accounts estimated at 1,500 seized Evans. Accounts vary as to how the vigilantes entered the jail. According to one account, a crowbar was used to pry open the iron door of the corridor leading to the cells; another said bricks were removed from a wall; a third said the jail door was battered down; and a fourth said ropes or chains hooked to horses were used to tear down the jail's alley door.[79]

Carrying guns of all kinds, men filled the jail corridor. Two or three officers present retreated before the muzzles. Someone stuck a revolver into jailer E. H. Nichols' face, shouting "Kill him!" Fire chief John T. McNulty grabbed the weapon as its hammer fell on the skin between his thumb and forefinger. The move probably saved Nichols' life.

Evans stood in a cell in the rear of the four-cell jail. Several Black inmates in the other cells hollered: "Are you looking for the murderer? He's in that cell." Others called out, "Be sure to get the right man," pointing toward Evans. The kidnappers let Evans put on his clothes and shoes, then yanked him out. As he was hauled away, he said to his cellmates: "Boys, I am sorry you told on me." Men dragged him down the corridor to the alley, where they placed a rope around his neck.

Then began a procession from the jail at Fourth Street and Second Avenue South to Central Avenue, and then west on Central. Men, women, and children, some only partly dressed, poured out of hotels and guest houses along the avenue. Both the street and the sidewalks were full as the parade, grimly silent, marched west toward the Black section. A lighted streetcar followed the procession, and behind it was a line of automobiles, motorcycles, and bicycles. As the cars pulled into line, someone shouted, "Put out your lights!" and every headlight blinked off.[80]

At the head of the column trudged Evans, still stoic and silent, the rope around his neck. Eyewitness Luther Atkins recalled Evans' silence: "He never said a word. He knew that he was guilty, and he knew it was his time, and as far as I know I never heard him say any sound and everybody was quiet walkin' down the street. And everybody was determined to do one thing, and that one thing was to lynch that nigger, and that's what they did. It was just that simple. However pitiful it was and unlawful."[81]

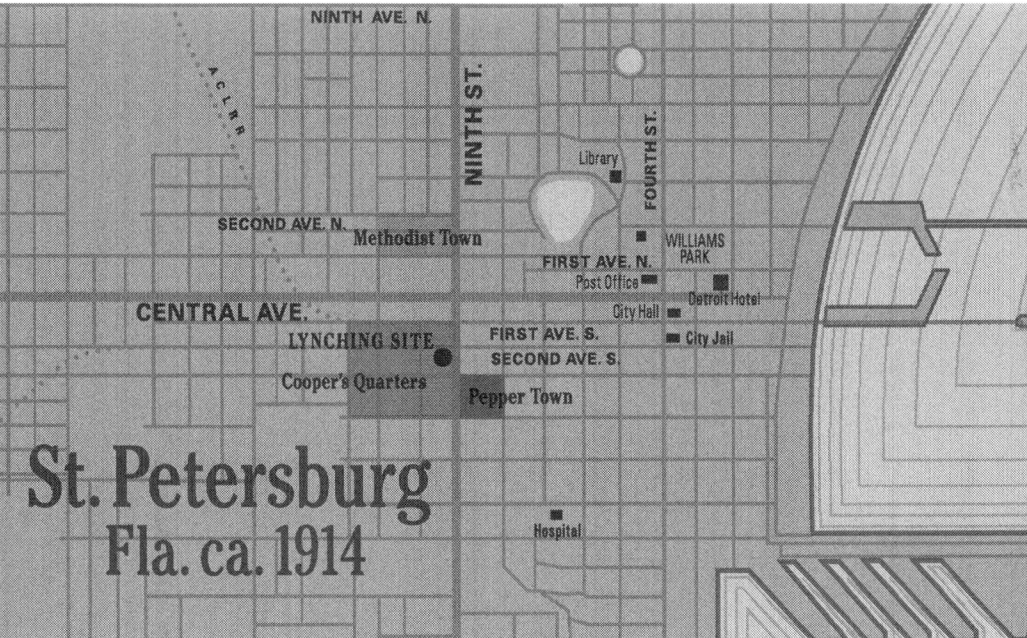

St. Petersburg's downtown was compact in 1914. The map shows Black neighborhoods and sites associated with the lynching of John Evans. Art courtesy of David Meek

The procession turned south on Ninth Street and moved to the corner of Second Avenue South where there was an electric light on an arm attached to a pole. Some in the crowd wanted to set Evans on fire, but as the rope was already around his neck, the leaders decided to proceed with the hanging. First, someone threw a rope over a trolley pole, but the mob leaders decided the pole was not strong enough. They moved across Ninth Street, thinking a tree there would do, but decided the street's east side was too dark. The crowd then went back to a light pole. A boy climbed up the pole's spikes and threw a rope over the crossbar, and as he did someone in the crowd fired a shot at him by mistake, missing. After he scuttled down, a few men started hoisting Evans off the ground. According to one newspaper account, Evans was pulled up three times but never cried out or made a plea for mercy.[82]

Women took lead roles

In every account of the lynching, both in newspapers at the time and by witnesses in later years, women played prominent roles in the episode. The *Times* reporter who covered the lynching recalled that a woman was one of the leading instigators. And as Evans desperately tried to wrap his legs around the pole while the white men heaved on the rope below, a woman in an automobile fired a shotgun into the Black man's body.[83]

The blast began a fusillade of bullets and shot. As Evans dangled in the noose, volley after volley erupted from rifles, pistols, and shotguns. Occasionally, a louder explosion was heard when someone pulled both triggers at once on a double-barreled shotgun. According to Luther Atkins:

"They shot that fella so fulla holes that I carried a postcard taken by a big flashlight. One of my friends here was a photographer, he took the picture at night after everybody left. You could actually see the holes in his body through his clothes. It was just riddled. Little kids with guns were shootin', and women standin' there shootin' and sceamin' and yellin'—and shootin'. It was the damnedest mess you ever heard in your life, you never heard anything like it."[84]

It all took about forty minutes from the time Evans was taken from jail. When it was over, the crowd melted away, remarkably quiet as it dispersed, as though, remarked the *Times*, "it had been going to a funeral instead of coming from an execution of its own making." Behind them, the blasted corpse of John Evans swayed in the soft Florida night.[85]

John Evans's body dangled in front of a Black neighborhood on Ninth Street South for nearly five hours. Mayor J.G. Bradshaw tried to stop the sale of this postcard photo, saying its circulation would damage St. Petersburg. Photo courtesy of the St. Petersburg African American Heritage Association.

Secret

"I am aware that the recent occurrence has been sufficient to excite everyone, but the crime has in a measure been avenged."
—Mayor J. G. Bradshaw

Two grim possibilities loomed as St. Petersburg entered its third day of fear, Friday the 13th. Perhaps angry white citizens, searching for the second suspect, would continue to rampage. It seemed likely to happen. Muttering crowds still gathered on the streets, and their numbers increased toward evening. Ebenezer Tobin, held under tight security by Sheriff Marvel Whitehurst, was now believed with certainty, though with little or no evidence, to have been John Evans's partner. Whitehurst was thought to have spirited him to Tampa for safekeeping, but when rumors circulated that Tobin was still in Clearwater, a clamor went up to march on the town and seize him. There was also talk about invading Tampa, if necessary.[86]

Marvel Whitehurst, Pinellas County's first sheriff, saved Ebenezer Tobin from being lynched. Photo Courtesy of Heritage Village Archives and Library

The second possibility was that a race riot would explode. Some white residents were threatening to storm Black neighborhoods again, and angry Blacks were ready to retaliate. Both sides issued fighting words. Florida Governor Park Trammell sent a telegram to Clearwater, asking Whitehurst whether St. Petersburg needed more troops to maintain order. Officials declined, but an infantry company in Pinellas County stayed on alert in the armory.[87]

Mayor Bradshaw, in a prepared statement, pleaded with the town to remain calm. "I am aware that the recent occurrence has been sufficient to excite everyone, but the crime has in a measure been avenged. We cannot help things by undue excitement which might work grave injury to our city," Bradshaw said.[88]

An attempt to quench some of the mob fever came with the issuance of a report about Mrs. Sherman. Acting with police as a representative of the crowds, J. C. Blocker made this public statement: "While Mrs. Sherman is on the road to recovery, the woman is in no condition to be bothered for several days. In justice to her, the people should not insist on anymore [N]egroes being taken before her for two or three days. As might be expected after such an experience, she has a horror of the sight of a [N]egro. Naturally, this excites her and is detrimental to her."[89]

Sherman's lawyer arrives

William P. Walsh, Sherman's lawyer and business partner, arrived from Camden a few hours after a policeman cut down John Evans's corpse at 3 a.m. on November 13. Walsh visited Mrs. Sherman and began immediately to settle her husband's estate. St. Petersburg, meanwhile, had already settled one thing: The coroner's jury, summoned by Magistrate Addison Arnold, viewed Evans's body at S. D. Harris' undertaking parlor on Central Avenue and reached a verdict. Evans, the jury reported, had died at the hands of parties unknown. His death certificate, signed by Arnold, cited "lynching" and "shot" as the causes.[90]

Such verdicts citing "parties unknown" were typical of lynchings everywhere. A Black person would be killed, often after being tortured, and the white perpetrators would remain anonymous. Because Blacks were virtually powerless in terms of voting, holding public office, or serving on juries, the arrest, prosecution, conviction, and punishment for lynchers was almost unknown. Said historian Robert L. Zangrando:

"Local white sentiment condoned (the lynchers') actions; public officials, answerable to a white electorate, either cooperated with the mob or sought refuge in silence and inaction. As a result, coroner's juries repeatedly found that death had come 'at the hands of parties unknown,' a sham verdict, indeed, since lynchers' identities were seldom a secret."[91]

"It would be virtually impossible to find out now," said Raymond O. Arsenault, a history professor at the University of South Florida St. Petersburg. "But the fact that half the white community was complicit in this makes it less important to figure out if there was any leader."[92]

That night it rained, as if to cleanse a troubled town. The showers sent milling crowd members scurrying into their homes. Armed patrols— composed of businessmen, according to a *Times* headline— stayed on guard to stop any stragglers determined to create disorder. Gradually, a calm descended.

On November 13 during the day, 179 Black women and children left on an afternoon boat to Tampa, and still others took trains out of town and smaller boats to Pass-a-Grille. But Saturday, November 14, found the town drifting back to routine. Business in stores and shops, practically at a standstill the past few days, began to recover, although saloons remained closed until Monday at the order of the mayor. The excitement and high emotion of both Black and white residents began to subside. The Pinellas County Teachers Association decided to hold its meeting as scheduled, while the city government and the Board of Trade met to discuss public ownership of waterfront property. And the *Times* carried a brief announcement: There would be a Sunday concert on the pier at 3 o'clock; a collection would be taken up to pay for band uniforms.[93]

Rushing to justify

Almost immediately, efforts began to justify or minimize the lynching of Evans. Prominently displayed newspaper stories said St. Petersburg Black residents were certain that Evans was guilty. Mrs. Sherman, whose mind had apparently cleared, was quoted as being sure that Evans was the man who had killed her husband and assaulted her. This was on November 14 after she had twice failed to identify Evans, and the day after she had been reported in no condition to identify suspects.[94]

Newspaper opinion pieces also took up the cause of justification. The *Times* carried a commentary that appeared first in the *Ocala Evening Star*:

"The (N)egro John Evans, who was lynched in St. Petersburg Thursday night, abided awhile in his passage through this world in Marion County, and was sent up by the superior court to serve a term in the penitentiary for grand larceny. The officers here say he was a bad character, and it was probably safe for the people of St. Petersburg to lynch him on general principles whether he was guilty of the crime he was accused of or not." However, the Florida State Archives did not find a record for Evans in its prison registers. Perhaps the *Evening Star* used mistaken terminology and Evans had been incarcerated in a county jail.[95]

The *Independent* dismissed Evans as an outsider:

"It should be remembered that John Evans was not a St. Petersburg (N)egro; he came here only a few weeks ago from Dunnellon. It is usually the (N)egroes who stray in here and stay only a short while who commit crimes. The bulk of the St. Petersburg (N)egroes are honest, straight-walking people who are industrious and well-behaved."[96]

Defending mob action was a common response after a lynching. Arthur F. Raper, research secretary for the Southern Commission on the Study of Lynching in the 1930s, pointed out that those who participated in or accept lynchings tended to be adamant that the right person was killed. He wrote:

"The credibility of the lynchers or pro-lynchers in taking at face value all rumors, and the development of the tradition of the absolute guilt of the mob's victims are both phases of the inability of the mass of white people to deal dispassionately with situations involving actual or potential racial conflict."[97]

In Evans's case, it made no difference that the evidence and accusations were circumstantial, questionable, or motivated by self-interest. Mrs. Sherman twice failed to identify Evans as her attacker, even as the man stood in front of her. If she had named Evans, her identification could have been called into doubt because she lay seriously injured, emotionally traumatized, and under medication. Moreover, Mrs. Sherman could not see without her glasses, which had been broken, and her doctor said the assault had further impaired her vision. Although there is no evidence to support it, Mrs. Sherman may have been persuaded to name Evans after his death as an attempt to rationalize the lynching.

As for the Black cellmates who insisted on Evans's guilt, it would not have benefited them to claim his innocence. The whites wanted a person they could consider guilty, if not Evans, then another Black person, either one of Evans's cellmates or someone still free in the Black community. As a relative newcomer to St. Petersburg, Evans was available for sacrifice by Black people who hoped to make certain that they themselves would remain safe.

Nor could compelling physical evidence be brought against Evans. The bloody shirt and shoes, which allegedly belonged to him, were discovered at least twenty-four hours after the crimes in a house where Evans was not living. A resident of the house expressed doubt that the shirt did, in fact, belong to Evans. The shoes could not be said with certainty to fit because, during Evans's second interrogation in the woods, posse members had simply jammed the shoes on his feet. Even a perfect fit would not have established his ownership or that he wore them the night of the Sherman killing.

Evans's own actions should be considered, too. A guilty man, once released, would be expected to hide or leave the area. Evans did neither. He took work west of town and refused to run even when he knew a band of men was coming for him again. After being recaptured and tortured, he still would not confess.

Perhaps the most damaging evidence was a pair of cuff links discovered later. The shotgun identified as the murder weapon was reported stolen from a Central Avenue house on Halloween night, and the cuff links were said to have been taken from the same house that night. However, they were not found among items reportedly belonging to Evans until after he was killed.[98]

'To protect the women . . .'

The actions of St. Petersburg's white citizens fit another aspect of segregated society in the South: that of the manhunt. Although statistics proved otherwise, whites thought that Blacks were prone to commit crimes against white women and that unless a Black was lynched periodically, women in remote areas would be in danger. Casual conversation years later suggested the lynching was carried out "to protect the women."[99]

According to Arthur Raper, "These assumptions underlie the traditional practice of Southern white men in arming themselves unofficially and hunting down an accused person. This method of mutual aid in policing an area evolved on the frontier and persist[ed] in localities where the populace, for whatever reasons, insist[ed] upon dealing directly with crime and criminals."[100]

In St. Petersburg, the mobs clearly fit the custom of providing unofficial aid to the law officers. With no apparent qualms, Police Chief Easters encouraged a posse to hunt down Evans the second time, even telling the vigilantes where to look. Meanwhile, the spirit of cooperation was evident in the naming of one man, J. C. Blocker, to act as an intermediary between the crowds and the lawmen. With such encouragement, it is not surprising that people in the mobs felt free to act without restraint.[101]

Throughout the disorder, news accounts tried to distinguish between the unruly crowds in town and the manhunters that scoured the countryside, as if one were inferior and the other elite. Those in town tended to be labeled irresponsible, while the search parties in the bush were viewed as responsible citizens who deserved more respect.[102]

To be sure, the men who took Evans the second time may have operated separately from the downtown crowd from whom town leaders requested patience. But which element ultimately proved the more responsible (or brutal) is difficult to say. All distinctions may have been lost by the time Evans was lynched.

In fact, the notion of lynch mobs being composed of rabble has been proven a myth, considering hundreds of newspaper accounts nationwide that point out the participation of prominent people from every station and profession. Rather than a band of howling rustics, mobs were more likely to be a cross-section representing every status in the community.[103]

Fear, resentment, and hatred can affect people regardless of social standing, and those emotions may cause distinctions to be made along caste or class lines. If St. Petersburg's white people, for whatever reason, held Blacks in fear, the lynching somehow served to reassure them. "It was something that had to be done to protect our wives and children," remarked Luther Atkins, who spoke of the lynching years later. He suggested that Blacks had to be suppressed or they would take control of the community—a sentiment like the one expressed when the town held a white primary in 1913. Again, the attitude fit a wider pattern. Throughout the South, particularly after Reconstruction, lynching became the typical method of intimidating Blacks and maintaining the racial superiority sought by whites. The practice, or the threat of it, was used as a means of social control and to enforce racial division.

Done by design

Strong feelings or mere curiosity may have prompted some St. Petersburg residents to join mobs spontaneously, but newspaper accounts and witness recollections suggest that the Evans lynching was quietly planned.

Some in the community had financial reasons to want a person quickly identified as guilty and dispatched as soon as possible. For these people, a primary consideration would have been St. Petersburg's economy, which was on the verge of vibrant, good health but dependent on the promised support of eastern capitalists and tourists. In a single stroke, a man had been murdered and his wife brutalized—a couple from the Philadelphia area whose support St. Petersburg needed. Worse, northern newspapers were following developments, and the dead man's partner, himself a prominent personality from the Philadelphia area, was coming to St. Petersburg to view the situation firsthand. Clearly, something had to happen to calm the community; neither killers on the loose nor prowling armed bands would be attractive to the refined northerners that St. Petersburg hoped to impress.[104]

Rumor, bloody clothes, and a speculative press to further persuade an aroused public made John Evans a good choice for a satisfying solution. Besides, he was a transient, and a Black one at that in an era when people of color often were shown contempt. Few people would object to killing Evans, and St. Petersburg could then return to the matter of pursuing prosperity.

On the afternoon of November 12, following the recapture of Evans, several things happened that suggest planning. First, a policeman visited the white people living near the Black area immediately west of Ninth Street South and warned them. Stanley Sweet, a witness to the lynching who lived with his family on Tenth Street and Fourth Avenue South, later remembered, "A police officer came up there and told my dad, he says, 'You'd better plan on getting out tonight because there's liable to be trouble.'" Secondly, the coroner's jury, whose members acted officially several times but were never named in news accounts, convened that afternoon. The group had viewed the Sherman death scene and would later view Evans's corpse before deciding unknown persons had killed him. But on the afternoon of November 12, there was no apparent official reason to meet. St. Petersburg's official records do not contain records of a formal meeting of council members or investigators. But leaders doubtless discussed events in St. Petersburg. Meanwhile, during the afternoon, downtown crowds took on an uglier mood after some strangers joined it. None of this proves the lynching was calculated. It does suggest a degree of anticipation and instigation.[105]

Additional evidence of planning came from Walsh, the lawyer, who quickly learned details of the events. While settling Sherman's affairs, Walsh as a matter of course would have talked with St. Petersburg community leaders and others concerned with the dead man's estate and his wife's welfare.

On his return to Camden several days later, Walsh granted an interview to the *Camden Courier*. Most of it contained a description of the mob action and Evans's hanging, but Walsh disclosed an element that went unreported in St. Petersburg newspapers. Walsh revealed that Evans had been tried and found guilty during a secret meeting of a committee composed of fifteen of St. Petersburg's wealthiest citizens. They were not named and have remained "parties unknown," as have those who took Evans from jail, marched him down the street, placed the rope around his neck, and blasted his body with guns. The non-identification of those who murdered Evans is absurd on its face. Those who participated or witnessed certainly knew who led the mob and who joined it, and probably would have recognized outsiders.[106]

Spectacle

"Clearwater was crowded today as though for a circus."
—St. Petersburg Evening Independent

Charged with murder, Ebenezer Tobin was tried on September 17, 1915, ten months after John Evans was lynched. After brief testimony, the all-white male jury took just fifteen minutes to convict him. They were not about to take the word of a Black man over a white woman. Judge O. K. Reaves sentenced Tobin to die.[107]

Said to be Evans's accomplice, Tobin maintained his innocence to the end. On the day of his execution, leaning against the railing of a ten-foot gallows, he looked over a crowd of about fifty people. Sheriff Marvel Whitehurst had issued tickets to those who wanted to see Pinellas County's first lawful hanging, which was held October 22 inside the jail yard in Clearwater, the county seat. An estimated 2,000 more had come by wagon, train, and automobile to grab whatever vantage they could. Men, women, and children packed buildings and trees. Those on the train from St. Petersburg enjoyed a fine view, according to the *Independent*, which compared the crowd to that at a circus. The engineer stopped the train "and everybody on the engine and cars saw the [N]egro die," the newspaper reported. On the scaffold, a Black minister read the Twenty-third Psalm. Tobin looked composed and seemed unafraid as he waited.

Earlier that morning, Rev. N. L. Anderson and three other Black preachers visited Tobin, and the *Tampa Tribune* spoke with him. He was said to be not greatly worried but "not in good condition physically and seems to have lung trouble." The *Tribune* reported that he said: "To the public of Pinellas County, I am one man who has been sentenced to death by the judge. When I leave here today, I don't feel I will be a dead man, thank the lord. I feel all right with God, and I hope you will be sure that you are getting hereafter the right man to sentence to death. To the people of St. Petersburg, I don't feel that any of the men tried to live more honest than I did or were more honest than I am."

At 11 o'clock, Sheriff Whitehurst and several deputies escorted Tobin to the gallows. The lawmen had hoped Tobin would confess as his death loomed closer. But he uttered no such words. Instead, he mounted the scaffold and spoke to all who could hear.

"I want to say to the good white and colored people that you are about to assassinate an innocent man," he said. "I am being assassinated for a crime I know nothing about. I will stand on that trap as strong as I am standing now. I think nearly all the white people, and a great many of the colored as well, think that I am guilty. If it is God's will, I am ready to go."

It took a few minutes to secure arm and leg straps to Tobin, who was then placed on the trapdoor. Deputy Dan Marshall secured the noose around Tobin's neck and Sheriff W. C. Spencer of Hillsborough County placed a death cap over the condemned man's face. Whitehurst dropped the trap at 11:06. Three doctors, including a Black physician, pronounced Tobin dead three minutes later. His family refused the body, and it was buried in an unmarked grave. It was the last sad note in the life of a man who almost certainly was railroaded.[108]

Mary Sherman testifies

Tobin almost walked free: no trial, no conviction, free to go about his life.

Mary Sherman was reported to be traumatized and unable to travel from New Jersey, where she had retreated a few weeks before the trial. Several newspapers reported her ill health and lawyers speculated that without her testimony, Tobin would not be convicted.

A *St. Petersburg Times* article was typical. Under the headline "Black Fiend May Yet Escape Trial," the article said "The woman is now in a serious mental condition at her home in New Jersey and is unable to make the trip to appear against the [N]egro. As a result of the blow upon her head a blood clot has formed at the base of her skull and the pressure from this has seemingly affected her mind to a very serious extent." It echoed the comments James Daugherty, representing the Sherman estate, had made in January.

The article went on to say that it had not been determined how and when Tobin would be set free, and then concluded on a grim note. ". . . but the opinion is that if the [N]egro is ever set free, that it is certain that he will be trailed and if caught will meet the fate of John Evans."[109]

State Attorney M. A. McMullen persuaded Mary to return to Pinellas County with her testimony. She arrived by train on September 16 and McMullen met her. The two huddled for more than an hour in McMullen's office. Despite reports that Mary was not fit to travel or testify, the *Evening Independent's* "Rambler" column reported that a friend of hers had visited the newspaper's office and declared that Mary "has not lost her mind or is mentally affected in any way . . . Mrs.

Sherman's mind is as sound as it ever was, but her physical condition is not good." [110]

Tobin had gone to trial on September 17 lacking both a lawyer and the money to hire one. On the day of the trial, the court appointed Joseph A. Morris, 33, as defense attorney. Morris, recently married, had been in Pinellas for just a few months before the hanging. He worked without pay, but apparently was sincere in his effort to save Tobin. He requested a change of venue, saying he knew taking the case to another county would mean additional hardship and expense, but that he was willing to bear it himself in the interest of justice. Judge LeRoy Brandon denied the motion. In his closing argument, described as eloquent, Morris said the evidence pointing to Tobin could be construed as circumstantial.

Mary Sherman, in what was called convincing testimony said to lack malice, identified Tobin as one of the killers. She said the faces of Tobin and Evans were so vividly impressed on her mind that she would not forget either of them, regardless of the excitement or strain she might have been under. She said she was helped in her identification by a large kerosene lamp that was capable of lighting the yard several feet from the house.

Mary's demeanor was different when she identified Tobin as an assailant a few days after the murder of her husband. "I wish somebody would lend me a gun so I could shoot the brute. I would kill him right here in this office," she said.[111]

Meanwhile, State Attorney McMullen spoke of Tobin's financial problems, lack of friends, and his own sympathy for Tobin, but said jurors should decide on the evidence presented. Defense attorney Morris argued that Mrs. Sherman might have been mistaken in her identification because of confusion.

Tobin testified that he had been home with his wife all evening after 7:30 on the night of the murder and assault. He said he had not been fired by Sherman but had quit to work for another man. But he conceded that ten days afterward, he still was not working at a new job. Tobin also testified that he attended a funeral with a friend on the afternoon before the murder and went to the friend's house until coming home. Two defense witnesses were called to court, but they were not called to the witness stand. No one came forward to corroborate Tobin's assertions. The only other witness was undertaker S. D. Harris, who said Sherman's body was not moved until Harris prepared it for burial.

The defense did not raise the possibility that there may have been others who wanted Sherman dead. Sherman, after all, had earlier in his life testified against the men accused of murdering a state senator.

He likely made enemies while serving as a government agent. Even Mary Sherman might have been motivated to kill her husband.

The all-white male jury comprised J. W. Gordon, of Largo; J. H. Blakely, Safety Harbor; A. J. Hayman, Clearwater; J .H. Riggs, Ozona; S. S. Saunders, Dunedin; T. J. Fennell, Wall Springs; J. J. Couch, Clearwater; J. A. Walsingham, St Petersburg; W. M. Morely, Tarpon Springs; J. W. Mills, Dunedin; G. W. Anderson, Largo; and Charles Humphries, Clearwater. (Black men were permitted to serve on Florida juries starting in 1908, but such service was rare for many years. In Pinellas County, for example, just two Black people had served on a jury by 1944.)[112]

A mysterious move, said to be an attempt to save Tobin's life, developed about ten days before the scheduled hanging. Gov. Park Trammell sent Morris a telegram and the defense attorney immediately asked Judge Brandon to continue the case so he could go to Tallahassee. The judge agreed and Morris left town. But whether he met with the governor, and what was said if he did, remains unknown. St. Petersburg residents were reported to be "not at all pleased" that Morris tried to save Tobin, and Whitehurst read the black-bordered death warrant to the condemned man on October 11.[113]

'Choked and trembling . . .'

A *Tampa Tribune* reporter had visited Tobin in jail after his arrest a year earlier. He wrote:

"When first seen, Tobin was on his knees in his cell praying in a voice choked and trembling with emotion. The man's eyes were tightly closed, and the tears were running from them down his cheeks and falling on his closely clasped hands, held against his swaying body."[114]

A Sunday school superintendent at a Baptist church, Tobin appeared to be "unusually well-educated for one of his race," the reporter said. Tobin could not explain his arrest except to say that he had worked for Frank Sherman. Tobin had lived in St. Petersburg for about three years near Twentieth Street and Tenth Avenue South and said he had worked for several prominent St. Petersburg men, including real estate brokers Snell and Hamlett, and men he identified as E. Estess, Dan Herman, B. Johnson, and a Mr. Clem, whose initials he did not know. None appeared as defense witnesses.[115]

*** *** ***

Were John Evans and Ebenezer Tobin guilty of the crimes of which they were accused? Circumstantial evidence, speculation, and public panic led to Evans's lynching. The same weak evidence and an incomplete defense resulted in Tobin's legal execution. Morris did not significantly explore Mary's apparent mental problems. A thorough investigation might well have revealed other suspects. But there was no such thing. For example, no testing of blood evidence by a chemist was done, as it was in the murder of William Boone, noted in Chapter Three. Nor was the relatively new process of fingerprinting used in the Sherman case, although St. Petersburg police officer W. S. Lindsay was experimenting with it in 1914. Inconsistency surrounded the shotgun and footprints leading from the Sherman house. Early reports cited footprints leading north from the house along the railroad tracks; but a stolen shotgun, said to be the murder weapon, was found south between the house and the town.[116]

In the frenzy to dispatch John Evans and Ebenezer Tobin, authorities did not look closely at the men's acquaintances. Nearly a dozen other men worked on the Sherman property. Any one of them may have been motivated to rob, kill a man, and assault a woman. James Vann and George Washington, two who knew Evans, left town after the lynching. While it wasn't unusual for Black people to flee during the disorder, most soon returned. Washington stayed away for nearly two years, returning only when Sheriff Whitehurst brought him back from St. Augustine. Washington had sheltered Evans and was thought to have acquired and kept the money taken during the Sherman murder and assault.[117]

Frank Sherman made enemies, as his personal history shows. The railroad ran within a few yards of the Shermans' house, possibly providing convenient access or a means of escape. In fact, a schedule suggested a train passed the house about the time of night someone murdered Sherman. Outbound or inbound, it could have been traveling at a speed that could still allow someone to climb aboard or hop off before or after committing a crime. Perhaps it even made an unscheduled stop. Such things had happened before. Between 1898 and 1912, a serial killer using trains to travel murdered people across the nation, usually bludgeoning his victims.[118]

Mary Sherman herself should have been a suspect. She had motive, probable means, and easy opportunity. Reports offer no suggestion that authorities questioned her thoroughly about her husband's murder, and Frank Sherman apparently left no will, meaning his wife automatically inherited.

Childless, she had followed her much older, egotistical husband around the nation as he tried to realize an elusive dream while, if not precisely discouraging hers, at least putting them on hold. Mary was a smart woman and a photographer in her own right. Then she wound up in what was very nearly a frontier. She had few if any friends nor any social outlet. News accounts referred to Frank Sherman as the "popular photographer" while his wife remained in the background, despite a few newspaper ads touting her services. Isolated, perhaps resentful and fed up, Mary might have yearned for freedom—even if it meant getting rid of a contentious husband who controlled the couple's money, which may have been hard-earned and insufficient for them to live as they wanted. The Shermans placed numerous ads selling their things and even placed an ad to rent out a room while they were in St. Petersburg. In addition, women typically were not allowed to open their own bank accounts in 1914.[119]

A skeptic might raise an eyebrow at the property transactions that took place a few weeks before the murder. The Shermans sold sixteen lots in Wildwood Gardens to Walsh for $3,000, a sum equivalent to more than $80,000 in 2022. If Frank Sherman held back all or any of the money from Mary, it might have been her breaking point.[120]

What of the shotgun used to kill Frank? Such guns were so common that either the Shermans or their assailants easily could have acquired one. St. Petersburg was a "shooting city." A gun club on Sixth Avenue South held well-attended weekly competitions. At one, "more than 50 ladies visited the grounds," according to a report. The crowd that followed Evans to his lynching carried lots of weaponry. From somewhere or someone in well-armed St. Petersburg, Mary easily could have acquired the means to murder.[121]

As for opportunity, Frank was an easy target, tucked in bed sleeping when he was shot dead. His situation does raise a question. If he was well into slumber, either Mary or another assailant could have shot him from inside the house. For some reason, the killer chose to shoot through a window.

Presumably, Dr. Wilcox examined Mary for evidence of sexual assault, though the era's mores would have discouraged publicly reporting the results. What of her facial injuries? Available reports did not describe them in detail. A beating could have caused them, whether by an intruder or a brutal husband. Even the recoil of a powerful shotgun, poorly held, could damage a shooter's face.

Local newspapers did not mention the $75 found in Frank Sherman's trousers pocket after he was murdered. Sherman's mother, Malvina Sherman, noted it in a letter to a friend written weeks after the crime. If Evans and Tobin robbed the Shermans, it is possible that in addition to forcing Mary outside, they would have ransacked the house and found the $75. They did not, and the skeptic would cast more doubt on Mary's account.[122]

To be sure, these are theories. There is no direct evidence to substantiate them. Conjecture minus evidence regarding events more than a century old is interesting but cannot be taken as fact. Still, the larger point remains. Authorities and other leaders, including the newspapers, took for granted the word of a white woman and for convenience, sacrificed two Black men. They failed to mine for truth and thus failed to win justice untainted.

*** *** ***

Reaction among newspapers outside St. Petersburg was mixed. As noted earlier, the *Ocala Evening Star* thought it was good idea to lynch John Evans on general principle. The *Star* came close to celebrating the episode: "St. Petersburg has set the pace in lynching. Nothing like that auto parade that escorted the doomed nigger has been seen before, though Ocala had quite a lively series of benzine carts going out the Kendrick Road to a similar location two years ago."[123]

The *Clearwater Sun*'s reaction was more subdued and even seemed to take a certain pride in Evans's reactions. "It is said that when they asked him to confess and name his accomplice he laughed in their faces—in the face of a horrible death confronting him." The same editorial said: "But guilty or not guilty, those who took part in the lynching, will, in sober moments, reflect back on the incidents of that night and their consciences will cry out against the sin of taking a human life.

"And it will be many a long day before St. Petersburg will live down the act of lawlessness committed by its people within its own fair city."[124]

*** *** ***

Mary Sherman never returned to her house, to St. Petersburg, or to Florida after Ebenezer Tobin's trial. The 1915 New Jersey state census listed her as a photographer. She did not see herself as a powerless victim. She saw herself as someone who could continue to work, regardless of being traumatized. But by the federal census of 1920, a profession was not listed for her.

< *Mary Sherman never returned to St. Petersburg after testifying at Ebenezer Tobin's trial. This was the last known photo of her. It was taken in 1935 and shows her resettled in New Jersey. Photo courtesy of Peter Stemmer/ Bassriverhistory. blogspot.com*

After leaving the trial, Mary lived with one of her sisters and her husband in Camden for a few years until the sister died of Bright's Disease. During the Spanish Flu outbreak, she moved in with two widows in the town of Haddonfield, New Jersey and joined the United Methodist Church. Shortly after, she moved to Collingswood where she lived alone. By 1928, she had moved to Gloucester City, where she purchased land, built her own house, and lived there until the age of 74. She moved to New Gretna, New Jersey, to live with her oldest sister, Harriett. By then, Mary had lived longer in her own home than any residence she had shared with her husband or with her family in the Pine Barrens. She at last had her freedom to come and go. She was capable of living by herself regardless of the trauma she had endured in St. Petersburg. Upon Harriet's death, Mary moved into assisted living.

At the time of her death, the New Jersey newspaper recognized her as a long-term resident. She was said to be survived by no one, even though Laura, the youngest of the Platt children, was alive and living in an institution.

In Camden's Harleigh Cemetery, where the poet Walt Whitman is interred, Mary had a small, gray headstone erected over her husband's grave. On its front is a pretty design of three small thistles carved above the name Edward F. Sherman and the dates, 1857 to 1914. Mary had purchased plots for her husband, for herself, for her husband's youngest brother, and for his wife. Mary, who in 1957 died at age 90 of the infirmities of old age, is buried among them. But she has no marker to show her final resting place. Her name is not listed under husband's name. She was not mentioned in any of her former in-laws' obituaries. The Mount Holly, New Jersey, welfare fund paid for her coffin. Mary must have exhausted her funds because when she died, she was living at Ancora, the state mental hospital, in New Gretna, New Jersey, which opened in 1955.[125]

Her existence might not have been notable if not for the murder of her husband and the man who was lynched because of her accusation.

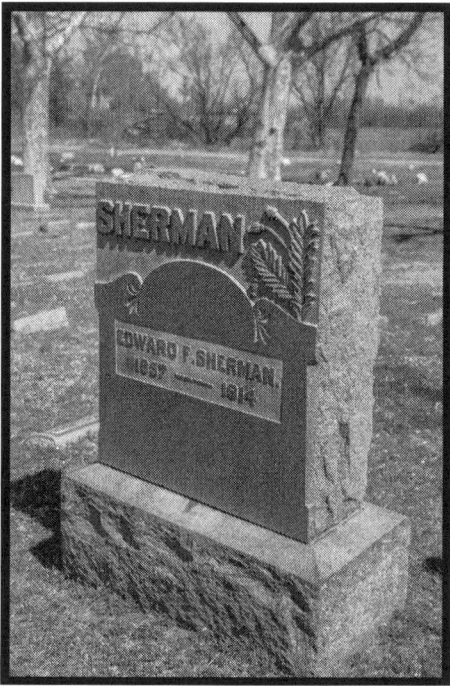

Frank Sherman is buried in Harleigh Cemetery in the family plot in Camden, New Jersey. So is Mary Sherman, but there is no marker for her grave. Photo Courtesy of Susan Beard

*** *** ***

The Shermans' St. Petersburg homestead of Wildwood Gardens was subdivided into many parcels. Eventually the house they lived in was moved and renovated. A newer dwelling stands on the site at this writing, next to an auto parts yard.

*** *** ***

Sheriff Marvel Whitehurst, who saved Ebenezer Tobin from lynching, as he did another Black man in 1917, was removed from office in

1920. A group of Pinellas residents petitioned Governor Sidney Catts to do so. Among their complaints was that Whitehurst had protected Tobin. "I protected Tobin because I thought it was my duty to do so until his guilt was proven—and I protected him from would-be lynchers in St. Petersburg," the sheriff said in the *St. Petersburg Times*. Citizens also complained that Whitehurst had not acted quickly to arrest a clique of confidence men operating in Tarpon Springs, and that on the sheriff's watch, a deputy had been accused of stealing jewelry from a Cincinnati couple found dead in their room from asphyxiation. Twenty-six prominent St. Petersburg businessmen signed the petition, among them William L. Straub and Lew B. Brown, whose newspapers often had lauded Whitehurst's performance in earlier years. The deputy, W. L. Strickland, escaped custody and was said to have fled to Havana, Cuba.

In 1921, Whitehurst sued *Independent* editor Brown and his son Chauncey Brown for $50,000, claiming a critical editorial in the newspaper had libeled him, but in 1923 a jury found in favor of the editors. Whitehurst ran for the office twice more but was badly defeated both times. But the dashing sheriff always had devoted admirers. One of his campaign ads read: "Marvel Whitehurst is a fighter. He isn't afraid of anything from wildcats to blind tigers . . . Like almost every fighter, Marvel doesn't look like a fighter at all. He has a mild and kindly eye, a pleasant smile and an air of non-combativeness which make him seem one of the least aggressive of men . . . his general appearance is that of a philosopher rather than a fighter."[126]

Two strokes, a week apart, killed Whitehurst in 1930 when he was 63 years old. He died at the Lake City soldiers hospital and Spanish American War veterans took charge of the funeral. Whitehurst had served with Troop A, Sixth Cavalry during the war.[127]

The passing of the first Pinellas sheriff, who served eight years in a county not far removed from its rough frontier days, was given only downplayed mention in the newspapers.

*** *** ***

Judge Leroy Brandon, who presided at Tobin's trial, moved to Hot Springs, Arkansas in 1930. He gave up the law and became a minister, dying in a sanitarium in 1934.[128]

*** *** ***

Joseph Allen Morris, the 33-year-old lawyer who defended Tobin, moved back to Georgia and practiced law in Atlanta. He also was publisher of the *Wayne County News* in Jesup, Ga. He died in 1948.[129]

*** *** ***

Judge O. K. Reaves, who sentenced Tobin to hang, retired from the bench and joined a prestigious Tampa law firm. He served as president of the Florida Baptist Convention. He died in 1970.[130]

*** *** ***

M. A. McMullen, who prosecuted Tobin, later served as a county attorney, state attorney, and circuit judge. He died in 1955.[131]

*** *** ***

William P. Walsh, the Shermans' lawyer, was a lawyer for the Camden County Society for the Prevention of Cruelty to Children and frequently defended youngsters brought to trial. He served as secretary of the Police Beneficial Association. As a younger man, Walsh took part in the Elks club "burnt-cork" minstrel shows. He died of heart disease in 1929 at age 50.[132]

*** *** ***

Most of the Black men rounded up by searchers scouring city and country were released. George Gadson, an early suspect, was sentenced to pay a fine of ten dollars—equal to $278.80 in 2022 purchasing power—or serve thirty days in jail for stealing George Meares' fruit.[133]

*** *** ***

Augusta Memorial Hospital, where Mary Sherman was taken after being injured, later became Mound Park Hospital, then Bayfront Medical Center, and eventually Bayfront Health St. Petersburg.

*** *** ***

The authors could not find a death certificate for Frank Sherman in Florida or New Jersey. Its absence appears odd, as Florida began statewide registration of deaths in 1899. But general compliance did not start until 1917, three years after Sherman's death.

Newspapers did not mention whether an autopsy was performed. At first glance, one would seem unnecessary because of Sherman's massive head wound. But a meticulous investigation might have demanded an autopsy to seek additional evidence, such as a sedative overdose or poison administered before the fatal gunshot.

*** *** ***

The two newspapers that published inflammatory articles while covering in detail the Sherman assaults, the lynching of John Evans, and the trial and execution of Ebenezer Tobin, enjoyed successful runs for years. Under Lew B. Brown and his son Chauncey Brown, the *Independent* flourished. Under different management, it fell on hard times in the mid-twentieth century. Then the *St. Petersburg Times* bought the *Independent* in 1962 and closed it in 1986. The *Times*, now called the *Tampa Bay Times*, won its fourteenth Pulitzer Prize in 2022. A city park is named after its early editor, William L. Straub, who helped to create the city's expansive public waterfront, much of it for many years off limits to Black people.

*** *** ***

In 2021, the City Council commissioned and accepted a university report on structural racism and the damage it has done to Black people living in St. Petersburg. To repair decades of harm to people of color, the council ordered creation of several programs in the areas of housing, health care, legal matters, and employment opportunities.

Afterword

By Jane A. McNeil

In the 1970s, as I rode my bicycle through my neighborhood of Snell Isle in St. Petersburg, I did not see children of color riding their bikes, playing in the backyard, or walking on the sidewalk.

The first time I met a Black girl my age was in my sixth-grade class at Canterbury School. During my school years in St. Petersburg, the murder of Edward F. Sherman, the lynching of John Evans, and the hanging of Ebenezer Tobin was not discussed in any of my classrooms. My parents did not lecture us about discrimination, race, or civil rights. My mother's side of the family was from a small town in Kentucky. When we visited them, we toured the Civil War sites. On these occasions, I do not recall any of my family's views on slavery or on the Confederacy that no doubt was on display at these historical sites. My family's own history as slave owners was never brought to my attention until I began researching my mother's side of the family. I doubt she knew or learned this from the paternal grandfather who died before she was born.

In Kentucky, my grandmother's best friend, a teacher, lived in a stately Georgian-style mansion on an old plantation dating back to the Revolutionary War. On a visit to her house when I was 12, I remember her pointing out the slaves' quarters in the basement of the house. There was a walk-in fireplace with a rocking chair next to it. The house was open to tourists. A "scene of slavery" was created for historical reference. Because the room appeared warm and inviting, as an impressionable child I did not question the number of slaves my grandmother's friend's family owned or how her ancestors treated them. Her friend reminisced about her family history, not the treatment of those enslaved. To these old Southern women, it was as if slavery was a passing phase in history, not one of the worst examples of human trafficking that was passively accepted in our country for 300 years.

During the civil rights protests from 1954 to 1967, my mother was a young wife and mother living in Ohio. Shortly before 1967, she and her first husband, along with my half-siblings, moved to Florida. By the end of the year, she would be divorced, remarried, and living in the Snell Isle neighborhood. After my twin and I were born in 1968, my mother enrolled in classes at St. Petersburg Junior College to earn her bachelor's degree. It was there in those classrooms she began to work on a dramatic play. At the public library, she gathered her research on the murder and the lynching while my sister and I read books in the children's section.

My mother's only comment on anything involving race was telling my twin sister and me never to use the "n" word. If we did, she said we would be showing our ignorance. I cannot say she actively fought for civil rights or took a stand in the community against local issues involving race, social injustice, and discrimination. She treated the Black women who worked with us with respect and often drove them home at the end of the day instead of asking them to take the bus. She died when I was 13, and her notes and files on her research were either lost or destroyed in the distribution of my parents' estate.

For her play, she chose an inter-racial couple for her main characters. In the late 1970s and early '80s, this type of relationship was taboo, especially in Florida. As a family, we watched Alex Haley's *Roots* like everyone else in America when it was televised in 1977. But I do not have a memory of any discussion after the series ended. Whether it was from her upbringing in Kentucky or my grandfather's shared experiences from being in St. Petersburg at the time of the lynching, she was inspired to write about the horrific event that many Pinellas County natives wanted to forget.

In her two-act play, *A Straw in the Wind*, my grandfather's character is a municipal court judge. He was not appointed judge until a year after the lynching. By 1918, he had left town with his wife and daughter to travel on a coal-mining expedition in South America. Reportedly, his friends and peers were shocked that he did not write or send a letter of resignation. My uncle, his youngest son, told me he joined the Navy at the end of World War I because of his guilt for not enlisting when many other men did. He would never practice law again.

Sometimes I wonder what he knew about the aftermath of the murder of Mr. Sherman and the evidence used to justify the lynching of Mr. Evans and the hanging of Mr. Tobin. He would have been privy to private conversations with the white men who were responsible for taking Mr. Evans from the county jail that night. What my mother or he knew, I will never know.

It was decades after my mother's death when I deciphered her play's real facts from the fictional. She used real names in some of the cast of her characters. The play's setting was in Destin, not St. Petersburg. It centered around an inn much like the Chautauqua Inn's boarding house where my grandfather and his second wife had resided when he first came to St. Petersburg.

As a young girl, my mother traveled back and forth with her family between Kentucky and Florida. At the time of her research, the only available resources of information, other than her father and the local lore she had heard, would have been from the Pinellas County courthouse records and the St. Petersburg Public Library. Personal computers had yet to be widely used, and I was not able to retrieve her taped dialogue or gain access to her personal notes, except what she underlined in Walter Fuller's 1972 book, *St. Petersburg and Its People*.

All information she used is still hearsay. She might have understood that Mary was not a grief-stricken widow from the newspaper articles written about her. She might have heard stories from older citizens in St. Petersburg who were alive in 1914 and remembered the lynching and the murder. What we do know is the lynching did not solve the problem of the white men's fears of the Black community's financial growth or the prejudice that preceded it. The hanging of Ebenezer Tobin reinforced the decision for many Black Floridians to follow the Great Migration to the northern cities. It also inspired the Black community to continue to fight for their voting rights, career opportunities, better housing, and higher education.

Today, the African American community is reclaiming its history. On February 21, 2021, a sign memorializing the lynching was permanently placed on St. Petersburg's Second Avenue South and Dr. Martin Luther King, Jr. Street (formerly Ninth Street South)

Like my grandfather, my mother wore many hats in her brief lifetime. Aside from being a novice playwright, she was a real estate broker, a travel agency owner, and a part-time college student. In 1967, when she met my father, she was young, beautiful, and a divorced mother of two working as a Realtor. My father was a prominent banker who needed to sell his house after his divorce to his first wife. When they eloped, she was three months pregnant with my twin sister and me. Shortly after they were married, my mother realized my father was a violent alcoholic. For her, he stopped drinking and promised to control his temper. However, their marriage was not a joyful union. My mother was a strong-willed woman, and my father was an undiagnosed manic depressive with possible post-traumatic syndrome as a veteran of World War II. When she decided to leave him on November 10, 1981, he killed her and himself when my sister and I were at school. He could not have known from her play, sixty-seven years earlier, Edward F. Sherman was killed on the same date.

Her legacy lives on in her play and through the Lily Foundation, a non-profit organization that serves women and children in need. As her daughter, it is my dream to give her script a voice. This book is the story behind the play. It is why I believe she was driven to write it, and why I have devoted a decade to researching it.

Thank you for reading, and thank you, Jon Wilson, for encouraging me to share authorship. Somewhere in the heavens, I would like to believe she is smiling and applauding our efforts to expose one of Florida's historical miscarriages of justice.

Endnotes

Introduction

1. Leonora Lapeter Anton, "A Lynching, Long Hidden in the Folds of St. Petersburg History," *Tampa Bay Times*, February 28, 2021. The *Tampa Bay Times* was known as the *St. Petersburg Times* until 2011. The latter designation is used for most references in this book. There also was a *Tampa Times*, which will be cited in these notes.

2. The editor is not named here because the conversation between the editor and co-author Jon Wilson was not recorded or otherwise documented.

3. Kevin Gannon, Twitter, July 5, 2020, retrieved April 25, 2022. Gannon is a history professor at Grand View University in Des Moines, Iowa.

4. The 1910 United States federal census provided figures for that year. Estimates of St. Petersburg's 1914 population varied: the St. Petersburg *Evening Independent* guessed 13,000 people lived in the town and immediately outside its limits, and the *St. Petersburg Times* guessed an area winter population of 25,000. Walter Fuller in his *St. Petersburg and its People* cited the 1915 Florida state census of 7,186. Limitsworldpopulationreview.com/us-cities/st-petersburg-fl-population, retrieved on May 20, 2022, provided figures for 2022. Florida's fifth-largest city in 2022, St. Petersburg approached 270,000 people, about 22 percent Black.

5. Taped interview with Lula Grant, December 2, 1981.

6. Anton, "Lynching Memorial Unveiled in St. Petersburg," February 23, 2021.

7. Anton, February 23, 2021.

8. *"Ken Burns: Being American means reckoning with our violent history,"* www.washingtonpost.com/opinions/2021/11/22/ken-burns-sand-creek-massacre-america-violent-history/, retrieved December 19, 2021.

Chapter 1

9   Robert L. Zangrando, *The NAACP Crusade Against Lynching*, 1909-1950 (Philadelphia: Temple University Press, 1980.

10 *Evening Independent*, March 13, 1914, and November 11, 1914; *St. Petersburg Times*, November 13, 1913, and November 12, 1914. Photography became more widely popular in the late nineteenth century, thanks to George Eastman's Kodak Company, which mass-produced cameras, according to the web site www.kodak.com/en/company/page/history, retrieved May 22, 2022.

11 *Evening Independent*, Nov. 10, 1914. Accounts of St. Petersburg's 1911-1914 period of real estate speculation are found in *The Story of St. Petersburg* (St. Petersburg: P.K. Smith and Company, 1948) and in *The History of St. Petersburg* (St. Petersburg: Tourist News Publishing Company, 1924), both by Karl Grismer, and in *St. Petersburg and its People* (St. Petersburg: Great Outdoors Publishing Company, 1972) by Walter Fuller.

12 *Evening Independent*, November 11, 1914.

13 *Evening Independent*, November 11, 1914; *St. Petersburg Times*, November 12, 1914. The *Times* said 9:30 p.m., the *Independent*, 10 p.m.

14 *Evening Independent*, Nov. 11, 1914. The newspaper quoted Mary Sherman as calling her husband Ed even though he was generally called Frank by family and friends.

15 Both the *Evening Independent* and the *Times* published detailed accounts of Mary Sherman's assertions about her husband's death and its immediate aftermath, including her flight for help. The Richters were longtime friends of the Shermans. J. W. Richter was a German immigrant who gained recognition as a talented photographer in Philadelphia before moving to St. Petersburg in 1912. He worked for Sherman in Camden. Four years after the murder, he suffered a heart attack and died in the water at Mitchell Beach, now Madeira Beach.

16 Elijah Gosier, "'20s Beach Boom Banished Blacks,'" *Tampa Bay Times*, Neighborhood Times section, February 12, 1990.

17 *St. Petersburg Times*, November 12, 1914.

18 lynching.cnsmaryland.org via www.axios.com, retrieved June 14,

2022. The Howard Center for Investigative Journalism and Capital News Service at Maryland's Philip Merrill College of Journalism collaborated on *Printing Hate*. The project also includes reporting from students at the University of Arkansas and Historically Black Colleges and Universities Hampton University, Howard University, Morehouse College, Morgan State University, and North Carolina Agricultural and Technical State University.

19 *Extra Judicial Killing of Black Americans*, cja.org/what-we-do/litigation/extrajudicial-killing-of-black-americans/, retrieved May 21, 2022. *Evening Independent, November 14, 1914.*

20 *The Negro Holocaust: Lynching and Race Riots in the United States, 1880-1950.* Yale Teachers Institute, https://teachersinstitute.yale.edu/ retrieved May 20, 2022. "The reason for the discrepancies in the figures is due in part to different conceptions of what actually constituted a lynching, and errors in the figures," according to the Teachers Institute. The Tuskegee Institute reported the 1914 lynching figures.

21 Ray Downs, "Florida Lynched More People Per Capita Than Any Other State, According to Report," *Broward Palm Beach New Times*. February 11, 2015. The article cited the Equal Justice Initiative *Lynching in America: Confronting the Legacy of Racial Terror*, (3d Ed. 2017). Retrieved May 21, 2022; lynchinginamerica.eji.org/explore/florida, retrieved May 21, 2022.

Chapter 2

22 The *Evening Independent* and the *Clearwater News* began on-the-spot coverage as soon as the search for suspects began. The *News* predated the *Clearwater Sun*, but the papers published concurrently for a while, including in 1914.

23 *Race and Slavery Petitions Project*, University of North Carolina at Greensboro, library.uncg.edu/slavery/petitions/about.aspx, retrieved April 5, 2021.

24 State Board of Health of Florida, Standard Certificate of Death, Florida Deaths 1877-1939; www.familysearch.com, retrieved May 29, 2022; federal census of 1900; *Evening Independent*, November 11, 1914.

25 Information about Ebenezer Tobin came from federal censuses of 1880 and 1900, both retrieved April 1, 2021, and from U.S. Civil War Pension Index: General Index to Pension Files, 1861-1934. Tobin's occupations were noted in the *Evening Independent*, November 11, 1914.

26 Venice, Calif., *Daily Vanguard*, November 23, 1914; Los Angeles City Directory, 1911; Los Angeles *Evening Express*, May 30, 1911.

27 Much of the biographical information in this section about Frank and Mary Sherman came from BassRiverHistory.Blogspot, Peter Stemmer, founder, and ancestry.com. The stolen watch incident was reported in the Camden, New Jersey, *Morning Post*, March 20, 1908. Frank's farming ambition was noted in the Wildwood newspaper, *Five Mile Beach Weekly Journal*, October 3, 1913.

28 *Delaware County Times*, Upper Darby Township, Pa., December 10, 1881.

29 St. Joseph, Mo., *Herald*, February 12, 1891. The "present administration" would have been that of twenty-third President Benjamin Harrison.

30 United States National Archives and Records Administration, Appointment Records, General Records of the Department of State, Box 111, Frank Sherman letter to E. W. Halford, February 27, 1889; Sherman letter to James G. Blaine, April 22, 1889.

31 National Archives, letter from John P. Brooks, Treasury Department, Secret Service Division, December 13, 1888. The "St. Alban's matter" was not further discussed.

32 Brooks letter.

33 National Archives. Frank Sherman was praised in several letters of recommendation, including those from Henry V. D. Schenk, agent, The Singer Manufacturing Company, December 27, 1884; A.H. Fetterolf, president, Girard College, January 19, 1889; E. A. Doty, adjutant, Post 76, Grand Army of the Republic, December 25, 1888; and George F. Penfield, president, Building Association League of Illinois, February 11, 1889. Sherman, upon a promotion, also received praise in the *United States Sewing Machine Times*, February 1887.

34 Mary Sherman earned a credit line as a photographer in the *Philadelphia Inquirer*, July 26, 1907.

35 Pinellas County Newspaper Index, Occupational Taxpayers in St. Petersburg, 1914, archive.org/details/WPA286502, 1938; newspaper archives at USF Libraries, Special Collections, University of South Florida, Tampa campus.

36 *Camden Morning Post*, November 25, 1907; archive.org/details/WPA286502.

Chapter 3

37 Browsing the advertisements in the era's Tampa Bay area newspapers gives the reader a sense of fashion. The ads of the time also offer a glimpse of popular culture.

38 *Evening Independent*, October 28, November 4, 5, 1914; *St. Petersburg Times* November 12, 1914. Descriptions of street paving and the trolley appear in the Grismer books and the Fuller book, and the *Times* periodically claimed twenty-five miles of trolley track. The *Independent* and the *Times* frequently published a list of the town's amenities under the heading "St. Petersburg has".

39 *St. Petersburg Times*, June 11, September 3, 1914.

40 Tampa, Fl., *Times*, May 23, 1914; *St. Petersburg Times*, May 20, 1914, September 3, 1914. The Boone case would pale after the Sherman murder.

41 *St. Petersburg Times*, October 1, 1914.

42 *St. Petersburg Times*, October 1, October 4, October 25, 1914.,

43 Grismer, *History of St. Petersburg*; *St. Petersburg Times*, May 19, 1906.

44 Nearly every edition of the *St. Petersburg Times* carried advertisements for steamship excursions. The McAdoo Bridge to Long Key, which became St. Petersburg Beach, was not opened until February 4, 1919.

45 The *St. Petersburg Times* named the baseball team the Burlies for manager Skeet Burleson. The team played its games at Sunshine Park on Coffee Pot Bayou. The league is not to be confused with the Florida State League, which began play in 1919. The 25 cents admission was equal to nearly $7 in 2022, according to https://www.saving.org/inflation/inflation.php?amount=1&year=1914, retrieved July 18, 2022.

46 The pier improvements were noted in many news stories in the *St. Petersburg Times*. Typical is an October 2, 1914, article. The newspaper consistently published announcements for card games.

47 *St. Petersburg Times*, November 3, 1914.

48 *Evening Independent*, October 28, November 5, 1914; *St. Petersburg Times*, February 3, 1914.

49 *Evening Independent*, October 24, October 29, October 30, 1914.

50 Advertisements for the businesses mentioned ran regularly in the *St. Petersburg Times*. The Willson Chase ad was published on October 2, 1914.

51 *St. Petersburg Times*, October 3, 1914; November 30, 1927.

52 African American neighborhoods in both the segregation and modern eras are mentioned by many sources. Ned Davis's contributions to St. Petersburg are noted in the *St. Petersburg Times* of December 8, 1928. Also see Marvin Simner, *Racial Segregation in the Rise and Fall of 22nd Street South: The Unfolding of the Historic Black Business/Recreational District in St. Petersburg, Florida*, Researchgate.net/publication/320774601, November 2017, Retrieved May 22, 2022.

53 Paul Barco, taped interview, November 24, 1981. Simner, ir.lib.uwo.ca/psychologypub/108/, Retrieved May 22, 2022.

54 Grismer, *History of St. Petersburg*; *Evening Independent*, June 24, 1913.

55 *Evening Independent*, June 23, 1913.

56 Barco interview.

57 *Evening Independent*, November 11, 1914; Grant interview.

58 *St. Petersburg Times*, October 4, November 1, November 19, 1914.

59 Grismer, *History of St. Petersburg*. The motto appeared on the Times' editorial page masthead for several years.

60 *Evening Independent*, October 28, November 5, 1914.

Chapter 4

61 *St. Petersburg Times*, November 15, 1914.

62 *Evening Independent*, November 13, 1914.

63 *Tampa Tribune, Evening Independent*, November 13, 1914.

64 *St. Petersburg Times*, November 17, 1914.

65 *Tampa Tribune*, November 13, 1914; *Evening Independent*, November 11-13, 1914; *St. Petersburg Times*, November 12-13.

66 *Evening Independent*, November 13, 1914. George Gandy Sr. was 63 years old at the time, so the person named may have been George Gandy Jr.

67 *Evening Independent*, November 12, 1914.

68 Ida B. Wells is credited with being America's most prominent opponent of lynching in the late nineteenth and early twentieth centuries. She wrote many articles and made many speeches on the subject. Those referenced here include *Lynch Law in America*, www.blackpast.org/african-american-history/1900-ida-b-wells-lynch-law-america/, retrieved April 11, 2022; Alex Tresniowski, lithub.com/how-ida-b-wells-brought-the-truth-about-lynching-to-national-attention/, *Literary Hub*, March 5, 2021, retrieved April 11, 2022.

69 *Evening Independent*, October 26, 1914.

70 *Evening Independent*, March 4, 1914.

71 *Evening Independent*, March 5, 1914.

72 *Tampa Tribune,* June 25, 1913.

73 *Evening Independent*, November 11-12, 1914.

74 Atkins interview.

75 *Evening Independent*, November 12-13; *St. Petersburg Times*, Nov. 13, 1914.

76 *Tampa Tribune*, November 13, 1914.

77 *St. Petersburg Times, Evening Independent*, November 13, 1914.

78 *St. Petersburg Times*, November 13, *Tribune*, November 11, 1914.

79 *St. Petersburg Times, Tampa Tribune, Evening Independent*, November 13, 1914; Atkins interview.

80 *St. Petersburg Times, Evening Independent*, November 13, 1914*; Tribune*, November 19. These references note articles describing the scene

in the jail when Evans was seized.

81 Atkins interview.

82 *St. Petersburg Times, Tribune, Evening Independent*, November 13, 1914; Atkins interview.

83 Taped interview with Ralph Reed, retired reporter, December 5, 1981; taped interview with Stanley Sweet, January 18, 1982.

84 Atkins interview.

85 *St. Petersburg Times*, November 13, 1914; Atkins interview.

Chapter 5

86 *Tampa Tribune*, November 14, 1914.

87 *St. Petersburg Times*, November 14; *Evening Independent*, November 14; *Tampa Tribune*, November 15, 1914.

88 *St. Petersburg Times*, November 14.

89 *Evening Independent*, November 13, 1914.

90 *Evening Independent, St. Petersburg Times, Tampa Tribune*, November 13, 1914; Evans's death certificate., Florida State Board of Health.

91 Zangrando, *The NAACP Crusade*.

92 Anton, *Tampa Bay Times*. February 28, 2021.

93 *St. Petersburg Times*, November 14-15; *Tampa Tribune*, November 14, 1914.

94 *Evening Independent*, November 13-14; *St. Petersburg Times*, November 14-15, 1914.

95 *St. Petersburg Times*, November 17, 1914; email from Florida State Archives to co-author Jane A. McNeil, October 7, 2020.

96 *Evening Independent*, November 14, 1914.

97 Arthur F. Raper, *The Tragedy of Lynching* (Montclair, NJ: Patterson-Smith, 1969).

98 *St. Petersburg Times*, November 15, 1914.

99 Atkins interview.

100 Raper, *The Tragedy of Lynching.*

101 *Evening Independent,* November 13, 1914.

102 *Evening Independent,* November 12, 1914.

103 Donald L. Grant, *The Anti-Lynching Movement 1883-1932* (San Francisco: R&E Research Associates, 1975).

104 The *Philadelphia Bulletin* and the Camden, NJ *Courier* provided continuing coverage of the violent events in St. Petersburg.

105 Minutes, City of St. Petersburg, Book 6, pp. 499-500; Sweet interview; *St. Petersburg Times,* November 13, 1914.

106 *Camden Courier,* November 20, 1914. Years later, surviving witnesses talked about participants and indirectly identified some.

Chapter 6

107 *Tampa Tribune,* September 18, 1915.

108 The crowd that came to see Ebenezer Tobin hanged, and Tobin's final minutes and statements, were reported in the October 22 *Evening Independent* and the October 23, 1915 *Tampa Tribune.* It is not known why Tobin's relatives declined to claim his body and let it go to a burial ground for indigent or unidentified people, often known as a "potter's field." Dr. Evelyn Phillips may have offered a clue in her Foreword to this book.

109 *Evening Independent,* January 30, 1915; *St. Petersburg Times,* May 7, 1915.

110 *Lakeland Evening Telegram,* September 16, 1915; *Evening Independent,* May 18, 1915.

111 *St. Petersburg Times,* December 4, 1914.

112 Tobin's trial was described in the *St. Petersburg Times,* September 18, 1915; the *Tampa Tribune,* September 14 and September 17-18; and the *Tampa Times,* September 18. The history of Black jury duty in Florida was described in floridajuryduty.com, retrieved May 21, 2022. Articles about early Black jurors in Pinellas appeared in the *St. Petersburg Times* of December 5, 1944, "Negro Serves on Pinellas Grand Jury as Court Opens; Criminal Case Dates Set," and of September 3, 1969, "'Historic' Convict Asks For Pardon."

113 *St. Petersburg Times*, October 15; *Tampa Tribune*, October 12, 1915.

114 *Tampa Tribune*, November 16, 1914.

115 *Tampa Tribune*, November 16, 1914.

116 *St. Petersburg Times*, May 29, 1914; June 5, 1914; *Evening Independent*, November 11-12, 1914.

117 *St. Petersburg Times*, June 6, 1916.

118 Bill James and Rachel McCarthy James, *The Man from the Train*, (New York City: Scribner, 2017).

119 The *Evening Independent*, February 21, 1913, for example, carries a Sherman add to sell; *The History of Women and Money in the United States in Honor of Women's History Month*, https://www.oneadvisorypartners.com/blog/the-history-of-women-and-money-in-the-united-states-in-honor-of-womens-history-month, retrieved July 24, 2022. Numerous other web sites note that women could not open their own bank accounts until the 1960s.

120 The lot sales were reported in the *Clearwater Sun* on November 19, 1914.

121 From 1910 through 1914, the *St. Petersburg Times* published more than 1,000 articles about gun clubs and shooting competition.

122 Pottsville, Pennsylvania, *Republican*, February 8, 1915.

123 *Ocala Evening Star*, November 14, 1914.

124 The *Tampa Tribune* of November 17, 1914, reported the *Clearwater Sun* commentary.

125 Co-author Jane A. McNeil twice made personal visits to the Harleigh Cemetery in Camden, New Jersey, where she looked at records and the Sherman gravesite. One of the visits was with photographer Susan Beard, who took photos of the gravesite on April 14, 2022.

126 *St. Petersburg Times*, May 14, 1916. A "blind tiger" was an illegal saloon.

127 Sheriff Marvel Whitehurst's military service, his role in Ebenezer Tobin's hanging, and his own death are reported in the *St. Petersburg Times*, May 14, 1916, March 31, May 12, and October 31, 1920, and October 15, 1930; the *Tampa Times*, October 15, 1930, and the *Tampa Tribune*, December 13, 1923, and October 15, 1930.

128 *Tampa Tribune*, September 19, 1934.

129 *Tampa Tribune*, September 3, 1948.

130 *Tampa Tribune*, August 23, 1970.

131 *St. Petersburg Times*, May 11, 1955.

132 Camden, New Jersey *Morning Post*, March 14, 1929, and December 12, 1925; the Camden, New Jersey *Courier-Post* of September 11, 1925, reported the "burnt-cork" shows in a looking-back column titled "The Peppery Pot."

133 Minutes of the Circuit Court, Pinellas County; *Tampa Tribune*, September 22, October 19, 22-23, 1915; *Evening Independent*, October 22, 1915; *St. Petersburg Times*, October 23, 1915; *Dollar Times*, www.dollartimes.com/inflation/inflation.php?amount=10&year=1914, retrieved May 26, 2022.

Acknowledgements

To paraphrase, it takes a village to create a book. The co-authors would like to thank numerous people and organizations who graciously helped during the writing of *Days of Fear*. Detailed accounts in newspapers furnished the heart of the story, primarily from the *St. Petersburg Times* (now the *Tampa Bay Times*), the *St. Petersburg Evening Independent*, and the *Tampa Tribune*. Several other newspapers published information pertinent to the narrative, and they are mentioned in endnotes.

We are proud to be associated with St. Petersburg Press, which agreed to partner with us in this project. Special thanks to Amy Cianci, who patiently guided us through the details of book production.

University of South Florida St. Petersburg professors Dr. Raymond O. Arsenault, Dr. Steven F. Lawson, and Dr. Gary R. Mormino provided inspiration and continuing encouragement beginning with the earliest stages of this project.

We thank the people who agreed to read the manuscript prior to publication and who made helpful suggestions. They include Dr. Goliath Davis, former chief of police and deputy mayor of St. Petersburg, who also wrote this book's preface; Boyzell Hosey, deputy editor of the *Tampa Bay Times*; Dr. Evelyn Newman Phillips, anthropology department chair at Central Connecticut State University, who also wrote this book's foreword; Gwendolyn Reese, president of the St. Petersburg African American Heritage Association; Terri Lipsey Scott, a city administrator for 37 years and executive director of the Carter G. Woodson African American Museum in St. Petersburg; and Rev. Carlos Senior, pastor at New Hope Missionary Baptist Church in St. Petersburg.

Playwright Bill Leavengood's influence led to the collaboration of the co-authors

Dixon Gutierrez, archivist assistant at the Florida Photographic Collection of the State Archives of Florida, and Patricia Landon of Heritage Village and the Pinellas County Historical Society helped us collect photographs. The authors appreciate St. Petersburg Museum of History director Rui Farias and staff members Nevin Sitler, Jessy Breckenridge, and Marta Jones for their research help, as well as Kerrie Ballis of the St. Petersburg Public Library. Artist David Meek graciously helped several times with the map of downtown St. Petersburg. We thank Peter Stemmer, who founded the BlogSpotBassRiverHistory.

Without him, we would never have found the photos of Frank and Mary Sherman and a letter in Mary Sherman's own handwriting. We are also grateful to Kathi Johnston, manager of the Wildwood, New Jersey, historical society, who helped find photos of Frank Sherman's photography studios.

We thank St. Petersburg legacy personality Marvin Mosher and independent researcher Nick Reale for their research help, and Shelly Reale for constructing the website associated with this book.

The co-authors thank Leonora LaPeter Anton of the *Tampa Bay Times* and Waveney Ann Moore of *Catalyst*, who wrote articles about racism and the events of 1914 that both encouraged the co-authors and sparked interest among readers. Anton quoted Kiara Boone, deputy director of community education for the Equal Justice Initiative. Boone said discussions about lynchings create an opportunity for reflection in communities. "Ultimately it creates a symbolic reminder of the work that communities need to do going forward."

Drew Davis of the *Press-Sentinel* in Jesup, Ga., provided a lead about the lawyer who defended Ebenezer Tobin and Janet Royal of Jesup provided information about the lawyer. Michael F. Foley, master lecturer at the University of Florida's College of Journalism and Communications, offered a lead, as did Clint DeWitt, a well-read scholar and an Environmental Projects Manager in Asheville, N.C.

Finally, the co-authors offer grateful thanks to their spouses, Rory McNeil and Becky Wilson, ever supportive, always patient, and quick with advice if they sensed a sentence, paragraph, chapter, or idea needed reconsideration.

About the authors . . .

Each of this book's co-authors brings a different voice and perspective. Jon Wilson, encouraged by University of South Florida St. Petersburg history professors, wrote a 1983 article about the November 1914 lynching in St. Petersburg for the journal *Tampa Bay History*. The article was a linear description of the episode. Jane A. McNeil was inspired by Wilson's article to investigate the murder of Edward F. Sherman and the lynching of John Evans. She and Wilson shared research and decided to collaborate on a book that would shed light on what others tried to hide more than a century ago.

Wilson was born in Scottsbluff, Nebraska and moved to St. Petersburg with his family in 1956. He worked for thirty-seven years as a reporter and editor for the *St. Petersburg Evening Independent* and the *St. Petersburg Times* (now the *Tampa Bay Times*). After retiring from newspapers, he worked as Florida Humanities communications consultant for eleven years. Wilson holds master's degrees in journalism studies and in liberal arts from the University of South Florida St. Petersburg. He is the author or co-author of five books about St. Petersburg, and in 2021 received a Key to the City from Mayor Rick Kriseman for inclusive chronicling of the city's history.

McNeil, a playwright and philanthropist, was born in Winter Park, Florida and spent her childhood in St. Petersburg. She earned her MFA degree in Creative Writing at Rosemont College in Rosemont, Pa., and earned a Certification in Practical Theatre from Villanova University. Currently, she is working on the adaptation of her late mother's play, based on the incidents that took place in November 1914. Said McNeil: "If we bury the racial crimes of the past, those who were not held responsible will succeed from the grave in denying their guilt."

Made in the USA
Columbia, SC
12 September 2023